THE COMPLETE

PHANTOM
of the
OPERA

THE COMPLETE
PHANTOM
of the
OPERA

GEORGE PERRY

RESEARCH BY JANE RICE

SPECIAL PHOTOGRAPHY BY CLIVE BARDA

AN OWL BOOK
HENRY HOLT AND COMPANY
NEW YORK

Library of Congress Catalog Card Number: 87-45772
ISBN 0-8050-0657-5
ISBN 0-8050-1722-4 (An Owl Book: pbk.)

Henry Holt books are available at special discounts
for bulk purchases for sales promotions, premiums,
fund-raising, or educational use. Special editions
or book excerpts can also be created to specification.
For details contact:
Special Sales Director, Henry Holt and Company, Inc.,
115 West 18th Street, New York, New York 10011.

The publishers wish to express their gratitude to
Biddy Hayward of the Really Useful Group
for her generous assistance in the preparation of this book.

First published in hardcover by
Henry Holt and Company, Inc., in 1988.

First Owl Book Edition — 1991

Designed by Bridgewater Associates
Printed in West Germany
Recognizing the importance of preserving the written word,
Henry Holt and Company, Inc., by policy, prints all of its
first editions on acid-free paper. ∞

1   3   5   7   9   10   8   6   4   2

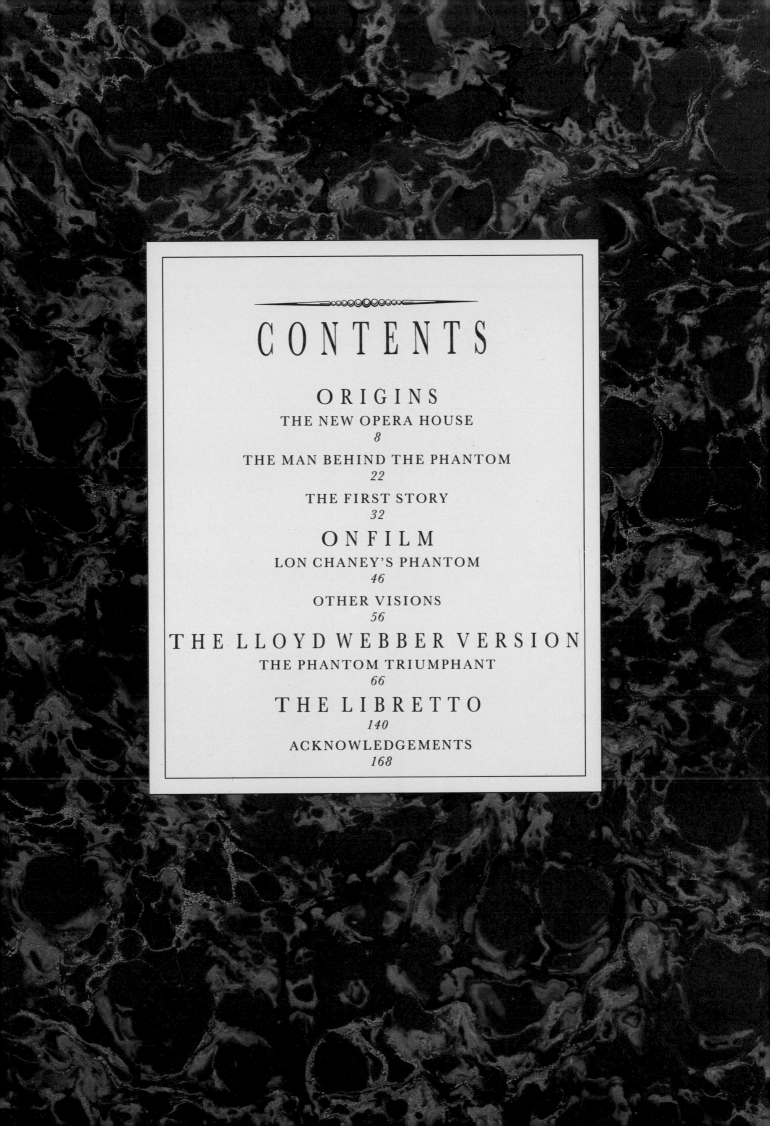

CONTENTS

ORIGINS

ON FILM

THE LLOYD WEBBER VERSION

THE LIBRETTO

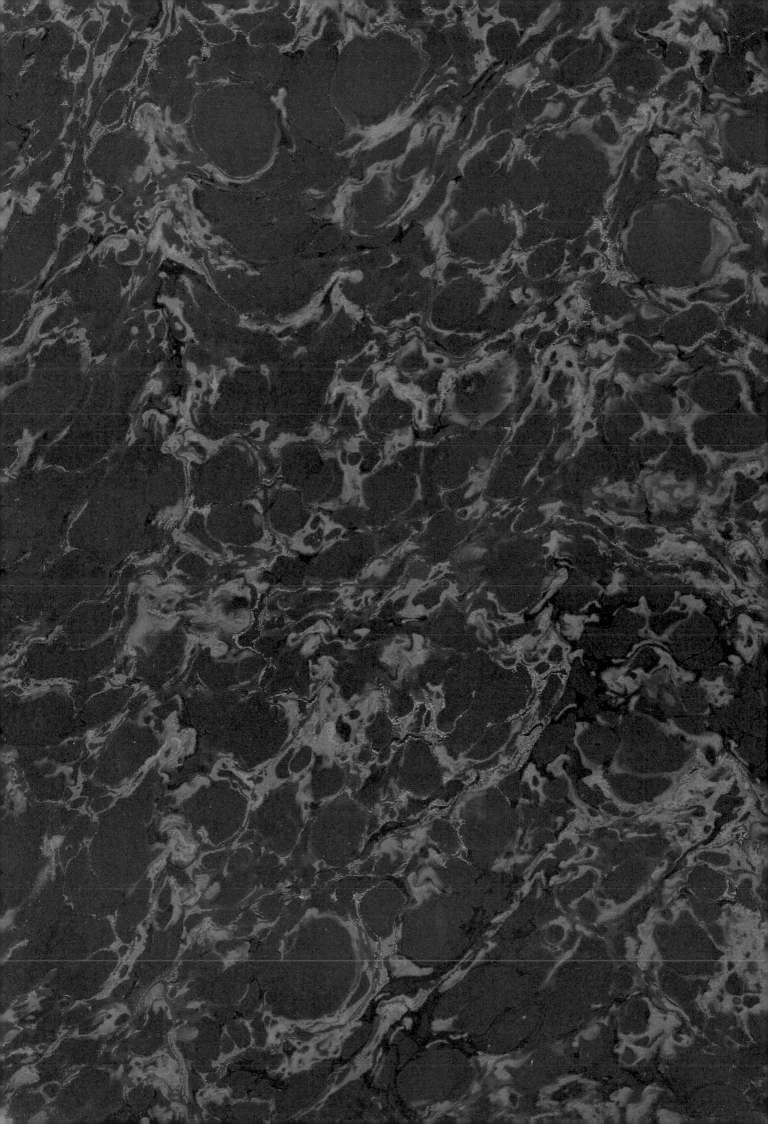

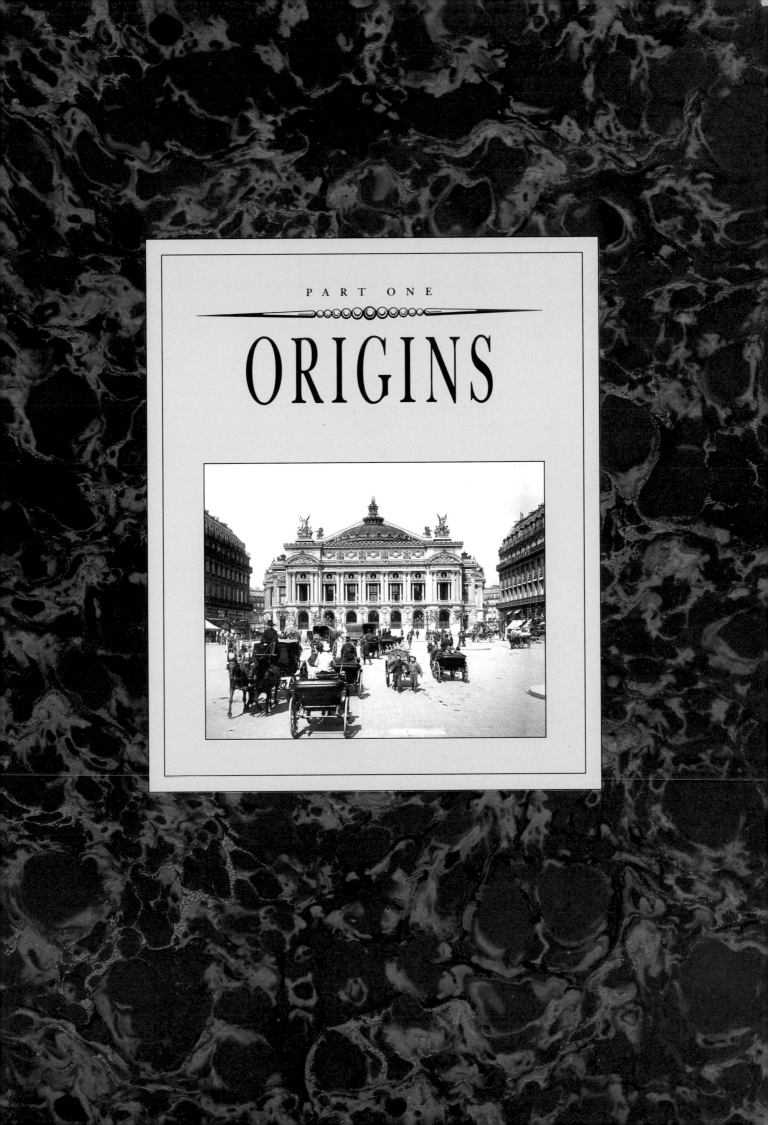

PART ONE

ORIGINS

THE NEW
OPERA HOUSE

*O*PERA is an inseparable part of the history of Paris. In 1669 Louis XIV founded the Royal Academy of Music, granting a licence to Pierre Perrin and the Marquis de Sordéac, 'to present, and have sung in public, operas and spectacles with music and in French verse'. Since then there have been thirteen opera houses. Some were borrowed, some were temporary, some were destroyed by fire, and some co-existed with each other. But it is Garnier's great building, opened in 1875, that has not only eclipsed all the others in its magnificence, but endures today as the only major edifice of France's Second Empire.

Baron Haussmann, appointed a prefect of Paris by the Emperor Napoleon III and nephew of Napoleon Bonaparte, was a city planner of genius. He was also granted draconian powers of demolition, and the shape of modern Paris with its broad, straight, tree-lined boulevards and avenues radiating like wheel spokes is a consequence of his singular vision. It was he who joined the Tuileries to the Louvre by destroying the intervening slums and extending the Rue de Rivoli. He built new bridges across the Seine, gave Paris a modern sewerage system and turned the Bois de Boulogne into a Parisian Hyde Park. In his projected layout of the new city, which he imposed over the street pattern of the *ancien régime*, he anticipated the presence of a great opera house worthy not only of the capital of France and the Second Empire, but of the culture of the world.

The popularity of the Emperor tended to be limited to the bourgeoisie. His penchant for continually involving France in foreign wars, and his neglect of the teeming working classes who had been forced to the edges of the city by the Haussmann reconstructions were eventually to prove fatal to the continuation of his shaky reign. In January 1858 Napoleon III made a visit to the opera house of the day in the Rue le Peletier, with the intention of hearing the singer Massol make his farewell performance. As his carriage drove into the narrow street there was a deafening explosion as first one bomb, then two more, were hurled at the royal procession. Although more than 150 people were killed or injured, including the coachman, the Emperor and Empress were shaken but unhurt. The perpetrator of the outrage was an Italian republican called Orsini. The Emperor bravely insisted on attending the performance, to appreciative cheers from the audience, but privately decided that a new building was called for. Haussmann was encouraged to draw up plans for a site near the Boulevard des Capucines, an area then being transformed, that would

Charles Garnier, the young and flamboyant architect of the Opéra. Of humble birth, he showed an early talent for drawing and mathematics. At the age of 17 he entered the Ecole des Beaux Arts where he won the coveted Grand Prix de Rome, enabling him to study for five years at the Villa de Medici in Italy. This classical training was to influence all his future work. In 1860, among 170 other contestants he won a competition for the design for the new Opéra. During its construction, he was renowned for his bouts of furious temper, and his singular looks made him an easy target for cartoonists. Garnier died in 1898, leaving behind him a few spectacular monuments to his genius, including the Casino at Monte Carlo and the tombs of Bizet and Offenbach.

be suitable for a superb new structure, an opera house that would not only be the envy of the world but would also have a special imperial side entrance that could be guarded properly.

Haussmann felt that this grand new opera house should form a focal point in his Paris plan, and he began to lay down broad new thoroughfares which radiated outwards in seven straight lines from the large square, the Place de l'Opéra, which was to be its setting. It was a part of Paris that had remained much the same as it was before the Revolution of 1789. The dense rabbit warren of old buildings and alleys standing in the way of Haussmann's scheme was ruthlessly flattened, although not without some criticism in the National Assembly from those concerned by reckless expenditure. The Avenue de l'Opéra struck out towards the Palais Royal and the Louvre. Demolition and construction had begun at both ends in 1854, but it was not until 1878 that it was finally possible to have an uninterrupted view of the largest royal palace in the world from the steps of the Opéra. The obstacle that had given Haussmann the most trouble was the Butte St Roch, a mound on which Joan of Arc had gathered her troops to attack the capital in 1429.

Thus Haussmann created his stately avenues and the *quartier* that has become the commercial hub of modern Paris, where luxury shops, fashion houses, airline offices and international companies congregate and various lines of the Métro system converge. The Avenue de l'Opéra, while not exactly another Champs Elysées, was the most important of Haussmann's diagonal thoroughfares and linked the rapidly developing business area adjoining the Gare St Lazare with the old heart of Paris around the Louvre and the cathedral of Nôtre Dame.

Initially, the sceptical citizens of Paris were bemused by the apparent vastness of the Place de l'Opéra, but Haussmann's intention was to make a dramatic setting in which to show off the eventual building, a sublime instance of a town planner providing a dramatic stage for an architect. Today, in spite of the swirling traffic, the view of the opera house from the corner of Boulevard des Capucines and its archetypal Parisian sidewalk café, the Café de la Paix, is a sight as unmistakably Parisian as the Eiffel Tower or the Arc de Triomphe.

It was not until December 1860, years after the idea had been mooted, that the Ministry of Fine Arts instigated a competition for a state-funded building worthy of the location. There were 171 entries, which is remarkable in that only a month had been available in which plans could be prepared. The judges decided after sifting through some 700 separate drawings that the outstanding ones were those of Charles Garnier, then thirty-five and a comparatively unknown architect. He had won the Grand Prix de Rome at the age of twenty-three, and had acquired a reputation for romanticism.

It was not quite a unanimous choice; the Empress Eugénie privately preferred the designs of France's most famous living architect, Viollet-le-Duc, who was a friend. Garnier had once worked for him. But Viollet-le-Duc did not even make the shortlist. The Empress examined Garnier's plans and, bewildered by the style, asked him what it was. Garnier, although ruffled and nervous, had the presence of mind to say, 'The Napoleon III style, ma'am.' What he was proposing was a vast building of traditional appearance in the fashionable neo-Baroque style of the Second Empire, but nevertheless one that would use the most advanced techniques of the day in its construction.

Work began on the site in the summer of 1861. Garnier's energy and ingenuity were quickly put to the test. Initial excavations revealed an underground stream running through the site which had the effect of turning the soil into mud, making it unstable for the laying of foundations. An engineering solution had to be found. For nearly eight months the local residents were driven mad by the pounding din of eight huge steam pumps working without pause, day and night, to dry out the saturated subsoil – in so doing lowering the water table sufficiently to dry up every well in the vicinity. Then Garnier built a double-layered concrete foundation sealed with bitumen to resist water seepage. The work was interrupted on 21 July 1862 when Count Walewski, the Minister of State, laid the foundation stone with due ceremony.

The building was conceived on a gigantic scale, and is still the largest opera house in the world. However, it can seat only 2,156 people and is now easily surpassed by others, such as La Scala, Milan, which can accommodate 3,500. But an examination of a cross-section of the building shows that the auditorium in fact occupies a relatively small space within. Even the stage itself covers a larger area, and the foyers and lounges, the Grand Staircase and other

Garnier and his design team create his dream of 'colour, faith and audacity'.

The secret underground lake where the Phantom made his home. A painstaking researcher, Leroux explored every inch of the Opéra before writing his novel. He remembered particularly the sinister lake in the depths of the building where he stumbled over the bones of a prisoner who had died during the Commune.

public parts of the building take up considerably more space than the tiered, horseshoe-shaped auditorium. The Opéra was conceived not merely for performances on stage but as a setting for grand state occasions, for galas and balls, festivals and feasts. It was to be a palace both for culture and society, a gathering point for the new middle classes where they could parade and show off their finery.

Such a building by necessity had to be big and equipped with copious spaces for promenading. Garnier used classical examples from the Renaissance as his inspiration: the colonnade by Perrault in the Louvre, the architecture of Palladio, Sansovino and Michelangelo. His work reflected his broad-based education, and like many a post-modernist of today he cloaked advanced engineering with the apparel of the past. The Opéra was built around a frame of ironwork, the structure supported on strong, fireproof girders at a time when such methods were relatively unknown. The great staircase would have been impossible had there not been a steel framework to support so much cantilevered marble.

The watery footings were turned to advantage. A lake was created deep beneath the stage area in the darkness of the fifth basement, and water from it was employed in the operation of hydraulic stage machinery. The lake remains to this day, although no longer used for that purpose. It acts, however, as an on-site reservoir in the event of fire, and every few years is drained so that the foundation structure

Garnier's great building, the thirteenth opera house in Paris since 1669, in a late stage of construction. The French capital is central to the history of opera. The dominant composer in the late eighteenth and early nineteenth centuries was Antonio Salieri, whose greatest triumphs were Tarare *and* Les Danaides, *performed prior to the French Revolution. His work was still in the repertoire after the opening of the Garnier opera house in 1875, although by the mid-nineteenth century Meyerbeer had succeeded him in popularity. An innovator, Meyerbeer was renowned for spectacular stage effects and in the 1849 production of* Le Prophete *he even introduced a roller-skating sequence.*

A cross section of the Opéra. Garnier was to combine architecture with the needs of the people experiencing it, providing them with a functional building of romantic opulence.

can be inspected. Normally there is only a couple of feet between the water surface and the brick-vaulted ceiling, but when the level is lowered there is plenty of room for the examination to be carried out from a boat.

Provision was also made in one of the lower basements for the stabling of twenty horses, which would be used in some of the more spectacular productions, and brought up to stage level by a gentle ramp.

The Opéra, as might be expected for so ambitious a design, took an eternity to build. The façade was unveiled in 1867. But there were hold-ups due to financial shortfalls when the government of the day drew in its horns. The eventual cost of the building was 47 million francs.

By far the most serious halt to the building works came with the short but brutal Franco-Prussian war of 1870. The defeat of the French army at Sedan brought the reign of Napoleon III to an end, the deposed monarch leaving for exile in England, where he would die before the Opéra would stage its first performance. A new republic was declared. Paris was once again in the throes of revolution, the fourth since Robespierre's Reign of Terror. The euphoria that greeted the declaration was swiftly overtaken by grim events. The siege of Paris began, with the city totally surrounded by hostile forces, and an attempt was made to oust the provisional government. There followed a brief but agonizing period in which the working classes rose up and declared the Commune of Paris.

The unfinished opera house building was taken over for use as an arsenal and a warehouse for storing vital food supplies (and a million litres of wine). There was not enough. Now Paris endured black days of siege, encircled by the Prussian army for nineteen weeks through a grim winter. The animals of the zoo were slaughtered and the carcasses sold to restaurateurs so that the rich could eat elephant meat, while the poor managed on dogs, cats and rats. Paris was on fire from German shelling, the people starved, and the streets ran with blood. At the point when hope ran out there was no option but to surrender. But shortly after the military occupation ended, members of the disbanded National Guard who were still armed took on the provisional government. Soon the Communards had an army of 100,000 men and cannon spread throughout sections of the city which had been shamefully abandoned by the politicians in the belief that the uprising would eventually peter out of its own accord.

The Opéra now performed the role of observation post, communications centre, powder store and military prison. In the dense labyrinth of stone stairways, underground passages and vaulted chambers of the basements there was ample room in which to incarcerate enemies.

The Communards were eventually smashed by government forces in a battle at the Père Lachaise cemetery. The last act of the Commune was the burning of major public buildings, including the Hôtel de Ville and the Louvre, where luckily only the library perished. But the bloody episode was a sinister pre-birth for Garnier's

The principal façade. 'I have adorned the monument with sections of marble, just as a vast and vibrant tapestry might be hung in the great spaces of a state room.'
Charles Garnier

great building, and in some of the Opéra's deep cellars, which seem to extend into the dark infinity of Piranesian voids, there is a perpetual chill that no amount of modern electric lighting seems able to dispel. It is easy enough to imagine that the first notion of the great building being haunted by tormented spirits took hold during the period of the siege and the Commune.

Another three years were to pass before the Opéra was ready to stage its first performances. The building, which had been conceived in the reign of Napoleon III, its foundation stone laid in 1862, was not inaugurated until France was well into its Third Republic. The gala opening was a signal that Paris had come fully alive again after the privations of four years earlier, and it marked the beginning of a glorious era of cultural excitement, elegance and high living that was to become known as 'La Belle Epoque'.

On 5 January 1875 the Grand Staircase was thronged with the first of many distinguished guests of the French government and the President of the Republic, Marshal McMahon. King Alfonso XII of Spain and his mother, Queen Isabella, were there, together with the Lord Mayor of London in his ceremonial chain and robes and attended by his sheriffs, swordbearer and halberdiers. Everyone present, some of whom had paid a thousand francs for their tickets on the black market, more than thirty times the official price, marvelled at both the gilded splendour and the breathtaking size of the building. They watched the Prelude to Auber's *La Muette de Portici*, Acts I and II of Halévy's *La Juive*, the Prelude to *William Tell*, an aria from Meyerbeer's *Les Huguenots*, and Delibes's ballet *La Source*. The musicians, as often is the wont in their profession, staged a modest form of industrial action in protest against what they felt was a cramped orchestra pit, and played so softly that they were almost inaudible. That flaw notwithstanding, the evening was a monumental success and the events on the stage, dazzling enough in their own right, were transcended by the rapture in which the building itself was greeted.

It was not even finished. Among the areas that still awaited the final coat of varnish was the special reception area that was to have been Napoleon III's salon, reached via a sweeping exterior ramp, but which was now to be reserved for the head of state. Today, this wing overlooking the Rue Scribe houses the Opéra library and the adjoining museum.

Covering a site of nearly three acres, or 118,500 sq ft, the new building stood seventeen storeys high (seven of them below street level) with basements so large that stage sets could be stored complete before being raised to serve their turn before the audience. The costume and property departments, workshops and other functional necessities were amply provided for. The flies soared several storeys above the stage. At roof level the Opéra was a romantic, spiky jumble of domes and cupolas, pinnacles and sculptures, offering the brave and hardy who had the stamina to make the unofficial climb a vantage point from which to look down on Paris.

The Opéra then had a permanent staff of more than 1,500 as well as two ballet schools, and even in today's budget-conscious climate around a thousand people are on the payroll. The Grand Staircase,

*E*xamining the 'sloates' on the stage of the Opéra.

*M*ephisto waiting below stage before being hoisted through a trapdoor. The inauguration of the Opéra (opposite), *on 5 January 1875.*

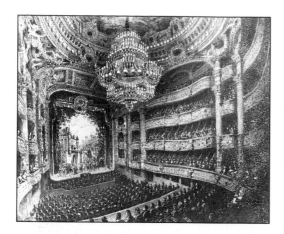

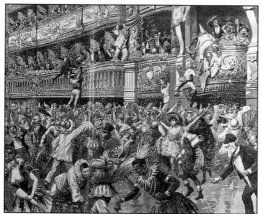

*M*asked Balls at the Opéra. Members of 'good society' only went to observe the wild behaviour of revellers on the floor – the wearing of masks allowing anonymity to everyone. The proceedings were described as like the Roman saturnalia or the Venetian carnival. The Masked Balls were, and still are, great crowd pullers. Immensely popular with visiting foreigners, the question often asked was 'Is French being spoken tonight at the Opéra Ball?' Right: The Grand Staircase.

The Armoury.

curving and bifurcating from the entrance hall into a double horseshoe in a magnificent marble sweep, leads to the main foyer, a huge mirrored room with a magnificent ceiling lit by ten crystal-laden chandeliers. On gala occasions the stairs are lined with helmeted and cuirassed troops of the Republican Guard, their blue and red uniforms and white buckskin breeches adding to the colour and glitter of the occasion.

The stage itself, 175 ft wide and 85 ft deep could be increased to a depth of 150 ft if the elaborately gilded dance salon immediately behind it was opened up. This extraordinary room, ringed with statuary and with sofas upholstered in crimson velvet, is dominated by an enormous St Gobain mirror 33 ft across and 23 ft high at its far end with a ballet barre in front of it. It was here that in Garnier's time the most favoured members of the audience were able to meet the dancers, and watch them limbering up. Balzac came here to observe, Degas to sketch. It was also a place where the season ticket holders could exercise an undue influence through their patronage on the manner in which new works should be performed, thus ensuring that no matter how splendid the building was, in terms of musical innovation the Paris Opéra had a reputation for insularity and mediocrity.

There were eighty separate dressing-rooms for the principal performers, plus a further eight large dressing-rooms for extras and orchestra, the biggest of which could accommodate two hundred people. There were more than 2,500 doors in the building which took the firemen over two hours to check. In Garnier's day there were 9,000 gas lights connected by over ten miles of pipe although, innovator that he was, he was anxious to experiment with the newly invented electric light. At the opening, electricity from a special battery room was used to set off bells and certain special effects projectors, and in 1881 the auditorium gasoliers were replaced by electric globes. At each end of the Grand Foyer the sculpted heads of women represent lighting methods through the ages: tallow, oil, gas, electricity.

Hanging in the centre of the auditorium – and today the centre-

The massive wooden capstans in the fly-loft (above), *used for raising backdrops. Marcello's Pythia* (opposite), *sculpted by the Duchess of Castigone Calonna, below the Grand Staircase.*

The Chandelier. Every two months the central circle of Chagall's ceiling is raised, a trap door in the floor of the Bailleau rehearsal room above is lowered, and the chandelier is lifted through to be cleaned and inspected by electricians.

Commissioned in 1962, Chagall's ceiling covers the original by Eugène Lenepveu. Chagall empathized profoundly with Garnier's architecture and said 'I wanted to reflect up there, as in a mirror, a handful of dreams, the creations of actors and musicians; to remember the swirling colours of evening wear below.' The ceiling is divided into five sections, each with a dominant colour in homage to two musicians and the operas they wrote.

piece of a colourful and decorative ceiling depicting various operas and ballets, painted by Marc Chagall – is the ornate crystal chandelier, seven tons of metalwork and glass, which was cut to Garnier's design, and later converted to contain four hundred bulbs. In 1896, during the concluding moments of the first act of *Thétis and Pélée*, with Rose Caron singing in full spate, there was a flash, a loud noise and a cloud of dust filled the auditorium, followed by fire in the ceiling. Had some anarchist hurled a bomb? The area was cleared and the injured rescued. A middle-aged woman was found crushed to death under the debris. What had happened was that a steel hawser holding one of the eight 770-kilo counterweights which kept the chandelier in position had been eaten through by fire caused by an electrical short circuit. The weight broke loose, fell through the ceiling and level 5, where no one was sitting, to land on seats 11 and 13 on level 4. The horrific accident aroused a sensational reaction in certain newpapers of the day.

It has to be said that Garnier's grandiose concept can be faulted. The eclecticism of the Opéra's architecture also represents a lack of originality. The stage layout was already outmoded by the time the building was finished. The external appearance from the Place de l'Opéra is squat and forbidding, a heavy effect intensified by the colonnaded loggia across the face of the building and the portico adorned by statues symbolizing the Muses. The composer Claude Debussy complained that from the outside it looked like a railway station, while within, the feeling was that of a luxurious Turkish bath. Théophile Gautier, on the other hand, saw it as 'the worldly cathedral of civilization'. Victor Hugo took this comparison a stage further by recognizing in Garnier's cruciform floorplan a sort of profane counterpart of Nôtre Dame.

It is without doubt an extraordinary fulfilment of the nineteenth-century romantic tradition in architecture, and an exciting monument of the era. The best view of it is from a quarter of the way down the Avenue de l'Opéra, where its massive bulk satisfactorily closes the vista. Garnier may not have fulfilled his ambition to create a distinctive architectural style for the Second Empire, but he did build a suitable memorial. There was no better setting for wealthy citizens to display that wealth, to such a degree that the spectacles on stage were sometimes a less arresting attraction than the opera-goers in their silks and jewels. The only other notable Garnier building that survives is the Casino at Monte Carlo. Its architect died in 1898, in what one can assume was a reasonably contented state of mind.

THE MAN BEHIND
THE PHANTOM

FITTINGLY, the author of *The Phantom of the Opera*, a classic tale of the bizarre, began his life unconventionally. On 6 May 1868 his parents were on their way from Le Mans to their home in Normandy, where his father, Julien Leroux, was a public works contractor. They had to change trains in Paris, and go from one terminal station to another, and were making the tedious journey across the city through streets congested with horse-drawn traffic. It had been their hope that the infant would not emerge from the womb until they had reached Normandy, but labour pains assailed Marie-Alphonsine and she was immediately rushed to a house where she gave birth to a well-formed baby boy.

Years later, when the child had become a young man, he returned to Paris to seek out the house in which he had been born. He found an undertaker's business in operation on the ground floor. His mordant comment was 'There, where I sought a cradle, I found a coffin.'

The Leroux's infant, christened Gaston Louis Alfred, was raised in Normandy, spending much of his time in the coastal village of St Valéry-en-Caux, where his family had shipbuilding interests. The boy loved sailing in the fishing boats and helping to unload the herring catch. He also became a proficient swimmer.

He was educated at the College of Eu, a Normandy grammar school, and developed a taste for literature, writing verse in his spare time. A star pupil, he frequently won prizes for his academic ability, and his teachers predicted that he would make a fine lawyer.

After acquiring his baccalaureate at Caen he was sent to Paris to begin law studies, but already he was writing short stories and poetry, some of which was published in Left Bank magazines. Triumph came when *L'Echo de Paris* published a sonnet sequence on the leading Parisian actresses and, although he had passed his law examinations and was called to the bar as a probationer, his heart was no longer set on a legal career.

In 1889, the year he gained his law degree, his father died and left him a million francs, a sizeable sum for a young man to have at his disposal. Young Leroux now succumbed to gregarious temptations and managed to squander the money on drink, gambling and unwise speculations inside six months.

In that period Paris, particularly the Latin Quarter, was a heady place for a young would-be writer, flush with new wealth and eager to play a poker hand. Leroux was the epitome of the bon viveur. His delight in good food, champagne and convivial company extended his

Gaston Leroux at the peak of his career as a journalist.

M. Gaston Leroux

waistline, and to counter his fuddled eyesight he habitually wore a pair of pince-nez, balanced as if by magic on the bridge of his nose. He was a sought-after companion and a genial host. Around his table the conversation was liberally endowed with wit and laughter. Only those who knew him really well were aware of a more serious side to his temperament, and of his preoccupation with the mysteries of death and its borderline with life, reincarnation and alternative existence.

Inevitably, as he ran through his fortune, which took him only a few months, he was eventually obliged to face up to realities. He had to accept that the dissolute life could not continue without an income, however valuable the experience and insight into human nature it had given him. He was also aware that the legal profession was not satisfying him. So he gave up the bar, where he had spent a dispiriting three years, and applied for a post on *L'Echo de Paris*, the paper that had already printed some of his verses.

Very shortly he was able to apply his new-found love of the theatre to dramatic criticism, and his legal training to covering courtroom events. One of his notable early reports was on the trial of Auguste Vaillant, an anarchist who had launched a bomb attack in the Chamber of Deputies. On the strength of it Leroux was immediately offered a better position on the important daily newspaper, *Le Matin*. This offered him scope for investigative writing, which was rapidly becoming his forte. On one occasion he achieved an extraordinary scoop by interviewing in his cell a prisoner who had been remanded for a serious crime, and was able in a brilliant article to demonstrate his innocence, to the discomfiture of the court officials and police. To secure his coup Leroux had resorted to a subterfuge of a kind considered unethical even by fellow journalists. He had claimed to be a prison anthropologist, and had even produced forged credentials to back up his pretence, an extraordinarily dangerous thing to do since he was running the risk of being caught and charged himself.

But the public was none too bothered with such finer points, merely enjoying a good story when it saw one, and soon Leroux was being acclaimed for his dramatic scoops and his exclusive interviews with celebrities. He had the knack of getting on with people, no matter how high or low their station, a considerable asset for a journalist.

There were, however, some aspects of the business of judicial reporting that he found distasteful. As a newspaperman he had been obliged to attend a number of executions by guillotine, the first being that of the wretched Vaillant, and these experiences made him a lifelong opponent of capital punishment in an age when such liberal thinking was somewhat advanced.

When he was given a job by *Le Matin* as a roving correspondent it was an exciting time, as modern communications were just beginning to revolutionize the business of journalism. He travelled far and wide across Europe and into Russia, Asia and Africa, frequently adopting incognitos and disguises to infiltrate his presence into the heart of what would turn out to be a good story. He covered the Kouropatkine offensive and the blockade of Port Arthur. He went with President Faure on a state visit to the Tsar. He reported the notorious second trial of Captain Dreyfuss, believing totally in his innocence. Writing on the acquittal, he said: 'This moment will stand out in the history of

The steps of the Opéra where, at any time of day or night, deals could be struck to buy a variety of dubious entertainment suited to the pockets and preferences of all social classes.

'L'Orchestre de l'Opéra' by Edgar Degas. During Leroux's time in Paris extravagant productions by Meyerbeer, Massenet and Charpentier were performed at the Opéra. The legendary eruption of Vesuvius was represented by showers of pebbles falling on stage.

justice, and future schoolboys should be no more be ignorant of it than of the date of the Battle of Actium or the coronation of Charlemagne.'

His adventures almost invariably resulted in colourful, dramatic and entertaining copy, and his articles enhanced the circulation of the newspaper to such an extent that Leroux himself became a celebrity. He was the readers' witness of great events, sometimes running risks to perform the role. He stood in the crater of an erupting Vesuvius. He saw Armenians slaughtered by Turks, and the Russians fighting the Japanese. Wearing the robes of an Arab he was the only European eyewitness of the riots in Fez. He observed the Black Sea mutinies, the rioting in Odessa and St Petersburg, and the bloody repression that followed. He revealed to the world that the Tsar had held a secret summit with Kaiser Wilhelm II in the Baltic, a scoop he acquired by ingratiating himself with a cook in the Russian court.

'No one can equal the reporter's zest for life, since nobody else possesses such a delight in observation ... The reporter watches on the world's behalf, he is the spy-glass of the world. Oh, how I love my profession!' he declared.

And then he threw it all up. His editor rang him at 3 a.m. shortly after his return from a long foreign assignment. Leroux was angry at being roused from a deep sleep and then being told to dash at once on a night train to Toulon, where a French battleship had been damaged in an explosion. 'Oh shit!' he bellowed down the phone, and hung up. It was 1907, and Leroux had decided at that moment to become a full-time novelist.

He had begun to write novels a few years earlier, a pastime regarded by his then wife, Marie Lefranc, with rather more tolerance than his dangerous journalistic career. Not that it was to save the marriage. It ended shortly afterwards in divorce, but in 1902 he met Jeanne Cayatte in Switzerland, and she was happy to become his live-in mistress in an age when such liaisons had to be treated with considerable discretion. In 1905 she even travelled to Russia with him while heavily pregnant. She was, however, a fluent Russian speaker, and served as Leroux's interpreter. But they were not to marry until 1917.

The first of Leroux's books appeared in 1903, to be followed quickly by three more. The first, *The Seeking of the Morning Treasures*, was serialized in *Le Matin* and aroused considerable interest in the more adventurous section of the readership. The story was based on the adventures of a real-life eighteenth-century robber, Louis Cartouche, who had left a number of caches of stolen goods dotted around Paris. They were still undetected when he was tortured and broken on the wheel in 1721. The newspaper saw to it that seven hoards, one worth seven thousand francs, the others three thousand francs, were planted in various places, and the astute reader could then indulge in some treasure hunting for himself – that is, if he was clever enough to interpret the clues contained within Leroux's narrative. It was an exciting stunt and it gathered much publicity, but not for the quality of Leroux's literary style.

It was, however, *The Mystery of the Yellow Room*, published in 1907, which justified his decision to give up journalism and concentrate on producing books. It was an early example of a locked room mystery, in which a murder is committed behind impenetrable sealed doors. The impossible crime was solved by a Gallic Sherlock Holmes of Leroux's invention, a detective called Joseph Rouletabille. He greatly admired two pioneers of detective fiction, Edgar Allan Poe and Sir Arthur Conan Doyle, but realized that in order to make his detective different he would have to present him with a problem more puzzling than anything that even Holmes had been called upon to tackle. *The Mystery of the Yellow Room* is not only the earliest Gallic example of a genre invented by Edgar Allan Poe with *The Murders in the Rue Morgue*, but also one of its most classic examples, worked out with an impeccable sense of logic. The detective Rouletabille was to appear in seven more of Leroux's novels.

His other major literary influences were the popular French novelists Stendhal, Dumas and Victor Hugo. He regarded Stendhal's *The Charterhouse of Palma* as one of the greatest adventure stories ever written. He wrote *The Mystery King*, which had a Monte Cristo theme, as his tribute to Alexandre Dumas. He also greatly admired Hugo's narrative construction in works such as *Les Misérables*. Leroux was a true enthusiast of the adventure novel genre, and

'B al du Moulin de la Galette' by Auguste Renoir. Café society in Paris. Never had a city provided so much inspiration for so many great painters – Impressionism, Fauvism, Cubism, Art Nouveau, all were founded during Leroux's lifetime.

ever ready to spring to its defence when it was attacked by the literary establishment. One of his books, *The Haunted Chair*, gave him an opportunity to hit back at the intellectuals of the Académie Française by making the successful candidate for the vacant seat an illiterate. Leroux used irony and pastiche as literary weapons, and sprinkled sharp-edged jokes through his works, some of which are now difficult to appreciate out of their period context.

In 1908 Leroux moved from Paris to Nice. The climate suited him, as did the proximity of the casinos. He was by now a relatively prosperous man of letters, although in spite of his prolific output he was never to become really rich. The gaming tables saw to that. But gambling was for him one of life's pleasures, and if he lost heavily he knew that he could draw on his writing talent to furnish another book and another publisher's advance with which to write off his debt. Thus he secured his place on the literary treadmill. 'I work only under contract,' said Leroux, 'I have to be pushed by deadlines.' His son later revealed that he had the disconcerting habit of signifying the completion of a manuscript by firing a loaded revolver from his balcony.

The growth of the public library movement in France immediately before the First World War brought him a large, but unprofitable readership, since it consisted of book-borrowers, not buyers. More calculated to bring him sales was the custom for teams of hawkers to stand at Métro entrances, handing out to all and sundry the first four chapters of a newly published work. Many of Leroux's books were promoted in that manner.

He was not merely a detective story author; his novels, published at the rate of at least one a year, embraced romance, fantasy and horror. Between October 1908 and July 1911 he produced five novels, one of which, *The Queen of the Sabbath*, was one of the longest ever written, being well over three hundred thousand words, or more than five times the normal length. He was also a playwright. Although his first work, performed in 1902, lasted for a mere ten performances, subsequent works enjoyed a more substantial success, including his own dramatic adaptation of *The Mystery of the Yellow Room*.

Somehow he seemed to be perfectly of his own time, and is now largely a forgotten figure. Hardly any of his books are in print, even in France, although when they first appeared they were very quickly issued in English translations. Several were made into films in the silent era and there were four productions of *Chéri-Bibi* and four of *The Mystery of the Yellow Room*, the latter two in 1930 and 1948, as talkies. His first screenplay, an adaptation of his novel *L'Homme qui Revient de Loin*, was written in 1916 for his neighbour in Nice, René Navarre, the actor famous for his portrayal of Louis Feuillade's master-criminal hero of the weekly serials, Fantomas, and who had become a film producer in his own right. In 1918 Leroux scripted a weekly serial for the Navarre company, called *The New Dawn*, and *Le Matin* published his own newspaper adaptation of the story.

In 1919 he formed a film company in Nice with Navarre and others, called Cinéromans. Leroux's actress daughter Madeleine performed in some of the subsequent productions. But, after a disagreement with the literary director of Cinéromans in 1922, Leroux lost interest in films. In any case by 1918 he had found his biggest ever reading public, and his greatest fame as a novelist. In one of his books, *The Infernal Column*, he coined the expression 'fifth column' which two decades later was to be applied to espionage activity in the Spanish Civil War and after that to spies in the Second World War.

But by now he had written the book which was to guarantee his immortality, even if the latterday public after his death would know little of its author, or that it was one work among scores of others. *The Phantom of the Opera* was published in 1911 and, surprisingly, attracted very little attention in the first weeks. Leroux claimed to have been inspired to write the story after visiting the Paris opera house, and roaming through its lower depths. In those labyrinthine cellars and the mysterious subterranean lake which was visible through iron grilles in the floor only if a torch was lit to pierce the blackness, there was an atmosphere that seemed to demand that a yarn be told. There were still visible traces from the period of the Franco-Prussian war and the Commune, when the place had been a prison, with various cellars transformed into dungeons. The prisoners held there had no chance of seeing the light of day, being far below street level. It needed little imagination to appreciate their plight.

Leroux also remembered the unfortunate accident of 1896 when one of the chandelier's counterweights had fallen on the audience, and the resulting horror. He tried to visualize the consequences of the chandelier itself dropping when the auditorium was full. He found that the long gestatory period of Garnier's building, which was under construction for fourteen years, offered certain possibilities, affording a well-placed person with a serious architectural background the time and opportunity to create within the complex honeycomb of passages and chambers all manner of secret routes which would be known only to himself. Thus he gave Erik, the Phantom, the training and vocation of an architect, as well as his passion for music.

Leroux began his book with an introduction in which he averred

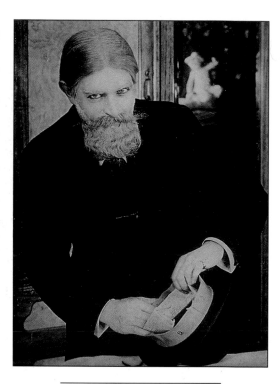

René Navarre in disguise in Louis Feuillade's film serial, 'Fantomas'.

The cover of the first edition of Leroux's novel.

that the Opéra ghost really existed. The subsequent narrative was based on that assumption, the author presenting his researches in a vivid and seemingly authentic manner. By using the devices of the journalist he assembled various documentary items and a mass of background detail, and gave the story a convincing air of verisimilitude. Leroux may well have invented the 'faction' style of novel writing in which real characters, events and places are interspersed with the fictional elements of the narrative with such precision that the join between truth and imagination is blurred to the point of invisibility.

The vast storehouse of experience he gained as a roving reporter was frequently called into play in his books. In his novel *Rouletabille with the Tsar*, he used as research his journalistic notes from his various visits to Russia on behalf of *Le Matin*. He also had a habit of occasionally putting himself in the narrative, as in *The Perfume of the Lady in Black* where he meets his famous detective, Rouletabille, face to face.

In *The Phantom of the Opera* he grips his readers from the very first words of the Introduction: 'The Opera ghost really existed. He was not, as was long believed, a creature of the imagination of the artists, the superstition of the managers, or the absurd and impressionable brains of the young ladies of the ballet, their mothers, the box-keepers, the cloakroom attendants, or the concierge. No, he existed in flesh and blood, though he assumed all the outward characteristics of a real phantom, that is to say, of a shade.'

Perhaps the vivid journalistic style is one of the reasons why Leroux's story fared better as newspaper serial material than as a hard-cover book. Newspapers in France, Britain and the United States carried it, and the accompanying graphic images of the Phantom seated at his organ or swinging on the chandelier gained readers' attention through the sensational manner of presentation.

The story, however, was typical of many other Leroux novels, in which a heroine was placed in extreme danger by a mysterious figure on the outside of society. To be fair, such a plot is one of the most basic there is. Leroux would not have been unduly disappointed by the lack of enthusiasm generated by the first appearance of *The Phantom of the Opera* in the bookshops, since by then he was well under way with the production of the next book. He was well used to the ephemeral celebrity that was associated with each of his publications at the time of their launch.

It is likely that *The Phantom of the Opera* would have become as neglected as most of his other works had it not been selected as a vehicle for Lon Chaney in 1924 and filmed by Universal in Hollywood. Both the film and Chaney's performance made an extraordinary impact.

When Leroux's daughter Madeleine was asked about her father in an interview in 1980, she recalled his kindness and good humour, and the regularity of the hours he spent at his writing desk. He was, she said, so gentle at home that it was hard to see how his books could contain so much turbulent material; whereas in public he could occasionally exhibit a short-fused rage. If, for example, a waiter had been inattentive, he'd swear never to set foot in the establishment again, only to be back a few days later, the incident forgotten.

With the Folies Bergère and Le Chat Noir at their height, it was not surprising that Paris became known as the entertainment capital of the world.

She also told how when she was making the film of *Tue la Mort* on location near Annot, a horse she was riding suddenly bolted away at full speed up a mountain road. A car giving chase only added to the horse's panic. She had covered a considerable distance when suddenly the horse was stopped by a brave man grabbing its bridle. She was astonished to see that it was her father, who had just happened to be there, quietly strolling down the track towards the location from the Annot railway station where he had arrived from Nice, having decided on a whim to go and watch the filming.

Leroux lived long enough to enjoy the renewed fame the film brought him in his last years. His final home, in the Rue Gambetta, was called the Palace of the North Star, a sumptuously baroque setting in which his imagination could be exercised to the full. He lived there happily and contentedly, relishing the joy of life, although by the time the film of *The Phantom of the Opera* was released his health was causing problems. On 15 April 1927, at the age of fifty-nine, he died unexpectedly from the effects of an acute attack of uraemia after an operation. He was buried in the Castle Cemetery, set high above Nice, overlooking the golden city and the azure Bay of Angels. His one remaining novel, *La Mansarde en Or*, was published posthumously.

THE
FIRST STORY

*G*ASTON LEROUX introduces his novel *The Phantom of the Opera* by asserting that the ghost really existed, and revealing how he had found the evidence for the thirty-year-old story he was about to tell when going through the National Archives of Music.

When I began to ransack the archives of the National Academy of Music, I was at once struck by the surprising coincidences between the phenomena ascribed to 'the ghost' and the most extraordinary and fantastic tragedy that ever excited the minds of the Paris upper classes; and I was soon led to think that this tragedy might reasonably be explained by the phenomena in question. The events do not date more than thirty years back; and it would not be difficult to find at the present day, in the foyer of the ballet itself, old men of high repute – men upon whose word one could absolutely rely – who would remember as though they happened yesterday the mysterious and dramatic conditions that attended the kidnapping of Christine Daaé, the disappearance of the Vicomte de Chagny and the death of his elder brother, Count Philippe, whose body was found on the bank of the lake that exists in the lower cellars of the Opéra on the Rue Scribe side. But none of these witnesses had until that day thought that there was any reason for connecting the more or less legendary figure of the Opera ghost with that terrible story.

He read documents, memoirs and talked to those who remembered the incidents that attended the kidnapping of a young singer, Christine Daaé, the disappearance of the Vicomte de Chagny and the death of Count Philippe. He tells how by chance he met the examining magistrate in the case, and learned of a mysterious witness known as 'the Persian' who claimed to have conversed with the ghost.

Leroux then relates how he tracked the Persian to a small apartment in the Rue de Rivoli, and interviewed him only five months before his death. The Persian produced documentary proof of the ghost's existence, in particular the letters of Christine Daaé, which Leroux compared with other examples of her handwriting to ensure that they were not forgeries. He then describes how workmen, digging in the cellars to bury phonograph records of famous artists for posterity, found a skeleton, at first believed to be a victim of the Commune, but alleged by Leroux to be that of the Phantom.

Leroux offers full acknowledgements to all those who had assisted him in the preparation of the narrative, including the architect in charge of the building, and a friend who let him delve in his theatrical library.

*S*tudy for 'Angel of Music' by Robert Heindel. Since his first exhibition in Atlanta, Georgia, American artist Robert Heindel has won recognition as 'the Degas of our time' through his studies of ballet dancers both in the USA and Britain. His 1986 exhibition, The Obsession of Dance, at the Royal Festival Hall, London, led to an extension of his activities into the field of the musical theatre when Andrew Lloyd Webber invited him to paint 'The Phantom of the Opera' in its pre-production stages, and also 'Cats' – already an established international success. After spending many hours observing, sketching, and taking thousands of colour slides, Heindel interprets his 'behind-the-scenes' look at the ballet and the stage musical in oils, pastels and conte crayon. His studio is an addition to his 300-year-old farmhouse near Easton, Connecticut where he lives with his wife, Rose.

Etchings showing characters from a toy theatre of 'The Phantom of the Opera' by Joseph Hope Williams, 1985.

Leroux then begins his narrative proper, taking the reader back to the 1880s, describing how the ballet girls chanced on a silent figure in dress clothes who had materialized backstage. It had been sighted many times before, and had become something of a legend. For where its face should have been was a death's head, or so it seemed – a yellow, noseless visage with black holes instead of eyes. But descriptions vary since no one has been close enough to make a proper inspection. The first chapter is largely backstage gossip by the girls, led by little Meg Giry, the daughter of the woman who looks after the boxes around the auditorium, who informs them that the ghost is allocated Box 5, and that he watches each performance from the shadows. She is interrupted by her mother who announces that Buquet, the chief scene-shifter, had been found hanged beneath the stage.

That evening Christine Daaé, a young singer, has just triumphantly sung in a gala performance which included the trio from Faust, taking the place of the diva, La Carlotta, who was ill. She is acclaimed by Philippe, the Comte de Chagny, and his brother Raoul, the Vicomte, who is twenty years younger and deeply smitten with her. They go backstage, where Christine has just had a fainting fit, and when she comes round Raoul reminds her of a childhood incident which took place when he first met her: 'I am the little boy who went into the sea to rescue your scarf.' She professes to be too unwell to continue the conversation.

Later, when the crowds have dispersed, Raoul is still lingering near her dressing-room door, and hears a man's voice within telling her

Characters from the 'Masquerade' scene.

that she must love him. When eventually Christine emerges in her furs she sweeps past him, alone. Raoul inspects the unlocked room and it is empty.

Leroux then speculates on the possibility that the ghost gatecrashed the occasion when the Opéra's two managers, Debienne and Poligny, had their farewell supper before handing over to their successors, Richard and Moncharmin. He presents the hearsay evidence speculatively, then describes in an extract from the memoirs of M. Moncharmin how the departing M. Poligny handed over a document in which the ghost demanded an allowance of 20,000 francs a month and a permanent box at his disposal for every performance. It was the reason why the two managers could no longer carry on. The ghost was too unreasonable.

The new managers decide to defy these requests, in spite of the possibility that Buquet's death had been caused by the ghost. It is, they feel, an elaborate joke, probably perpetrated by their predecessors, and when they receive a letter a few days later from the ghost, complaining that his box had been sold, they agree to let the old managers have it for the next performance sung by Christine Daaé. There follows a letter of thanks and a demand for the balance of his allowance from 'O.G.', as the Opéra ghost is wont to sign himself, and a letter from the ex-managers that they would not have dared to use the box at all. Annoyed, the new managers decide to allow the box to be sold for all performances. It leads to an evening being disrupted by maniacal laughter. Mme Giry is sent for, to see if she can shed light on

Etchings from the toy theatre.

the situation, and she tells the managers unequivocally that they have angered the ghost. She refers to other incidents where the ghost's presence has caused a disturbance. They take her for a madwoman and decide to dismiss her.

Christine Daaé seems strangely reluctant to sing, but she sends the Vicomte de Chagny a note confessing remembrance of the childhood incident with the scarf, and adds that she is paying a visit to Perros-Guirrec in Brittany, to her father's grave. Raoul dashes after her, recalling on the way how her father, a Swedish peasant with untapped musical gifts and a talented daughter, had been brought to Paris by Valerius, a music professor, then stayed in Brittany for the summer; how the daughter's scarf blew out to sea, and he, the boy Raoul, had

rescued it. Thereafter they had played every day until the autumn parted them. Her father died, and Christine drove herself to forget the young aristocrat, devoting her life instead to her art. But Raoul, in spite of her indifference, has watched her every performance at the Opéra.

'The End of Innocence' by Robert Heindel.

Surprisingly, she is waiting for him at Perros, and he asks why she has ignored him for so long. When he tells her how he heard a man speaking to her within her dressing-room, she becomes pale and frightened. Later, in the graveyard where her father is buried, she tells him of the Angel of Music legend, how she has been visited by him and been given lessons in singing from him. It is, she believes, the ghost of her father.

In the middle of the night Raoul follows her as she goes to the graveyard as if in a trance, and he hears perfect music which seems to draw him towards the grave. Then he is suddenly attacked by a spectre with a death's head, and brought back to the inn in the morning still unconscious.

Leroux then quotes from Moncharmin's memoirs an uneasy experience in which the two managers go to have a closer look at Box 5, and are both convinced they have seen something there – Moncharmin a death's head resting on the ledge, his colleague Richard a wan old woman's shape like that of Mme Giry. Bravely, they vow to watch that Saturday's performance of *Faust* from the box themselves. They then receive a stern letter from 'O.G.' demanding the restitution of his box, the replacement of Carlotta by Christine Daaé, the revoking of Mme Giry's dismissal, a further plea for his money, and the threat that if his terms are not met the house will have a curse on it.

While they are fuming at this latest impertinence the Opéra stable-keeper arrives to ask them to dismiss his workforce of stablemen because César, the prize among the dozen horses, has been stolen, allegedly by the Phantom. Then Mme Giry appears saying that she

*'Phantom Dancers'
by Robert Heindel.*

has had a letter from him, but before she can get any further she is literally booted out of the office by the indignant Richard.

Meanwhile, Carlotta is contemplating a threatening letter which says that if she insists on going on she will face a misfortune worse than death. A further letter urges her to have a bad cold. Suspecting a plot involving her rival, Christine, her resolve to perform hardens. She defies the instruction. But during the performance she suddenly loses her voice, emitting strange toad-like sounds.

The house broke into a wild tumult. The two managers collapsed in their chairs and dared not even turn round: they had not the strength; the ghost was chuckling behind their backs! And, at last, they distinctly heard his voice in their right ears, the impossible voice, the mouthless voice, saying:

'She is singing tonight to bring the chandelier down!'

With one accord, they raised their eyes to the ceiling and uttered a terrible cry. The chandelier, the immense mass of the chandelier was slipping down, coming towards them, at the call of that fiendish voice. Released from its hook, it plunged from the ceiling and came smashing into the middle of the stalls, amid a thousand shouts of terror. A wild rush for the doors followed.

The papers of the day state that there were numbers wounded and one killed. The chandelier had crashed down upon the head of the wretched woman who had come to the Opéra for the first time in her life, the woman whom M Richard had appointed to succeed Mme Giry, the ghost's box-keeper, in her functions! She was killed on the spot and the next morning a newspaper appeared with this headline:

**TWO HUNDRED THOUSAND KILOS
ON THE HEAD OF A CONCIERGE!**

That was her sole epitaph!

After the tragedy Christine disappears, and some days later an

anxious Raoul enquires of Mme Valerius, the widow of the music professor who had brought her late father to France, if she knows of her whereabouts. The elderly woman, now bedridden, tells him that Christine is with the Angel of Music, who lives in heaven and has her in his thrall. It is from him that she has been receiving singing lessons. Raoul is in despair, but a few mornings later a note arrives from Christine asking him to meet her secretly at the Opéra masked ball.

Narrowly avoiding a sinister scarlet-garbed figure with a death's head, purporting to be Red Death, and recognized by Raoul as his assailant at Perros, they go to a place where they can talk. Christine tells him that she must give him up. Disconsolate, Raoul hides in her dressing-room, and watches as she is addressed by a voice in the mirror, into which she vanishes.

The next day he calls on Mme Valerius and finds Christine with her. He tells her that he saw her speak to a man called Erik in her dressing-room, and she reveals that he is her Angel of Music. She makes him promise not to come to her dressing-room again, unless she sends for him. For the next few days their relationship is an uneasy one. Then they go to the roof of the opera house, and with Paris spread out beneath them Christine tells of how she was lured by the masked Erik to his lair in the depths of the building on the back of the missing white horse, César, and how his bed was a coffin. She describes how he played his composition to her, an opera called *Don Juan Triumphant,* and how she snatched his mask off to reveal a face of indescribable ugliness, how he confessed his love and resolved to make her a great singer, and how she was moved by pity. Unknown to Raoul and Christine, the Phantom is above their heads, perched on the statue of Apollo, and has been listening to every word of her betrayal.

As they leave the roof the Persian is standing at the foot of the stairs and suggests that they take a different route. Later, Raoul wakes in the middle of the night and thinks that Erik is watching him.

'I'm Here, I'm Here, I'm Here' by Robert Heindel.

'The Phantom of the
Opera' by Robert Heindel.

'The Phantom, Michael
Crawford' by Robert
Heindel.

Philippe tells Raoul that he should not marry Christine, regarding her ghost stories as a manifestation of madness, and he is concerned for the good name of the family. During a performance of *Faust* Christine suddenly vanishes on stage before the audience and there is speculation as to whether her disappearance is the work of Raoul or the ghost. Then Raoul arrives backstage and his distressed condition makes it clear that he is innocent. He accuses the unseen Erik, but is helpless to find the missing girl.

Leroux pauses in his narrative to describe how the managers, facing the demands of the Phantom for his allowance, place 20,000 francs in an envelope, only to have them substituted for false banknotes. They suspect that Mme Giry is responsible for the deception and accuse her. She is able to demonstrate they they are mistaken. Later more notes disappear, even though they have been attached to Moncharmin's coat by a safety pin.

The police are summoned to deal with both the missing money and the vanished opera singer. The theory is put forward that she has been abducted by Philippe to get her away from Raoul. Then the Persian reveals himself to Raoul as having a special interest in the Phantom, and tells him that Christine is with Erik somewhere in the opera house. He suggests they arm themselves with pistols, and then they go to her dressing-room, where the Persian shows how the mirror can become a door leading to secret inner passages. They go down into the cellars, holding their arms up as if ready to fire their pistols, a precaution urged by the Persian to counter the deadly effect of the Punjab lasso, the device already used to strangle Buquet. In the darkness of the lower basement they have a frightening encounter:

The fiery face came on, came on, gaining upon them. They could see its features quite clearly now. The eyes were round and staring, the nose a little crooked and the mouth large, with a hanging lower lip, very like the eyes, nose and lip of the moon, when the moon is quite red, bright red.

How did that red moon manage to glide through the darkness, at a man's height, with nothing to support it, at least apparently? And how did it go so fast, so straight before it, with such staring, staring eyes? And what was that scratching, scraping, grating sound which it brought with it?

The Persian and Raoul could retreat no farther and flattened themselves against the wall, not knowing what was going to happen because of that incomprehensible head of fire and, especially now, because of the more intense, swarming, living, 'numerous' sound, for the sound was certainly made up of hundreds of tiny sounds that moved in the darkness, under the fiery face.

And the fiery face came on . . . with its noise . . . came level with them! . . .

And the two companions, flat against the wall, felt their hair stand on end with horror, for they now knew what the thousand noises meant. They came in a troop, hustled along in the shadow by innumerable little scurrying waves, swifter than the waves that rush over the sands at high tide, little night-waves foaming under the moon, under the fiery head that was like a moon. And the little waves passed between their legs, climbed up their legs, irresistibly, and Raoul and the Persian could no longer restrain their cries of horror, dismay and pain. Nor could they continue to hold their hands at the level of their eyes: their hands went down to their legs to push back the waves, which were full of little legs and nails and claws and teeth.

Yes, Raoul and the Perisian were ready to faint, like Pampin the fireman. But the head of fire turned round, in answer to their cries, and spoke to them:

'Don't move! Don't move! . . . Whatever you do, don't come after me! . . . I am the rat-catcher! . . . Let me pass, with my rats! . . .'

The method of the opera house ratcatcher is to turn the light on himself to draw the creatures along the passageways.

Later, thinking they have reached the Phantom's lair, Raoul and the Persian lower themselves inadvertently into a torture chamber from which they cannot get out.

The Persian then takes over the narration, describing how previously he had found Erik's house beneath the Opéra on the other side of the subterranean lake, and how on crossing it in a boat he was pulled under and nearly killed. Erik used a reed to swim underwater and attacked him for intruding into his domain. The Persian reveals that he had known Erik in his own country, as a deformed person of superior intellect, and that now he challenged him over his obsession with Christine. Eventually the Persian returns with Raoul in their attempt to rescue the young woman, but they are trapped in the torture chamber.

Christine is imprisoned in the Phantom's quarters next door, and they are able to converse with her through the walls, but she cannot help them. Erik has an ornamental grasshopper and a scorpion in two

'*Phantom Rehearsal, Dancers*' by Robert Heindel.

'*Sarah and Michael, Music of the Night*' by Robert Heindel.

'*The Phantom, Michael Crawford*' by Robert Heindel.

boxes, and tells her that if she rotates one of them it will save the men, but if she chooses the wrong one the opera house will be destroyed. Meanwhile Erik turns up the heat in the torture chamber, making it so hot that both men fear they will be roasted alive, and they begin to hallucinate that they are in jungle and desert. Eventually, on the brink of death, the Persian finds a secret way out of the room, and they find themselves in another chamber full of barrels of gunpowder. Christine meanwhile, at the Phantom's urging, takes a chance and turns the scorpion. The room in which the Persian and Raoul are now trapped is flooded by a sudden torrent, and they are threatened with with drowning. The Persian's written narrative ends at that point.

The story is resumed by Leroux, who says that he heard it from the lips of the man in his old age, shortly before he died. The men had fallen unconscious after the flood, but the Persian wakes up in Erik's quarters, where Christine is ministering to him. Erik describes her as his wife. Later both the Persian and Raoul are returned to their homes. Philippe has been found drowned in the Opéra lake. Erik calls on the Persian and tells him that he is dying, and that Christine is the first woman to have allowed him to kiss her. He explains that the death of Count Philippe had been beyond his control, he had been trying to rescue his brother. Christine had persuaded him to release Raoul, and he would as a mark of gratitude to the Persian for his kindness hand over all the papers and artefacts relevant to her disappearance. Erik then left in a cab for the Opéra. Three weeks later an advertisement was published in *Epoque*: 'Erik is Dead.'

In an epilogue Leroux explains how the Persian was the only one to have known the whole truth. A visit to the aged M Poligny proved to be useless, and the Persian reminds Leroux that the manager had never realized the extent to which he had been duped by Erik. Erik had blocked up all the secret entrances to his house before his death, and it was never found, nor was the manuscript of *Don Juan Triumphant*. But Leroux did discover a secret trapdoor in the managers' office, which was how Erik had managed to abstract the money from under their noses. The Persian explained how Erik had been born a monster, the son of a master mason who lived near Rouen. His earliest memory had been of a mask being placed over his head in the cradle to hide his horrific features. He was exhibited as a freak at fairs, and travelled widely across Europe and Asia, already a gifted musician, practising ventriloquism and legerdemain. In Persia he became a master architect, brilliant at designing secret passages and trapdoors. In Paris he tendered for part of the opera house construction, and used some of his time on the site to build concealed passageways and a home where he could hide from mankind.

The reader knows and guesses the rest. It is all in keeping with the incredible yet veracious story. Poor, unhappy Erik! Shall we pity him? Shall we curse him? He only asked to be 'someone', like everybody else. But he was too ugly! And he had to hide his genius *or use it to play tricks with*, when, with an ordinary face, he would have been one of the most distinguished of mankind! He had a heart that could have held the empire of the world; and in the end he had to content himself with a cellar. Surely we may pity the Opéra ghost!

I have prayed over his mortal remains, that God might show him mercy, notwithstanding his crimes. Yes, I am certain, quite certain that I prayed beside his body, the other day, when they took it from the spot where they were burying the phonographic records. It was Erik's skeleton. I did not recognize it by the ugliness of the head, for all men are ugly when they have been dead as long as that, but by the plain gold ring which he wore and which Christine Daaé must have slipped on his finger, when she came to bury him in accordance with her promise.

The skeleton was lying near the little well, in the place where the Angel of Music first held Christine Daaé fainting in his trembling arms, on the night when he carried her down to the cellars of the opera house.

And now, what do they mean to do with that skeleton? Surely they will not bury it in the common grave! . . . I say that the skeleton of the Opéra ghost is no ordinary skeleton and that its proper place is in the archives of the National Academy of Music.

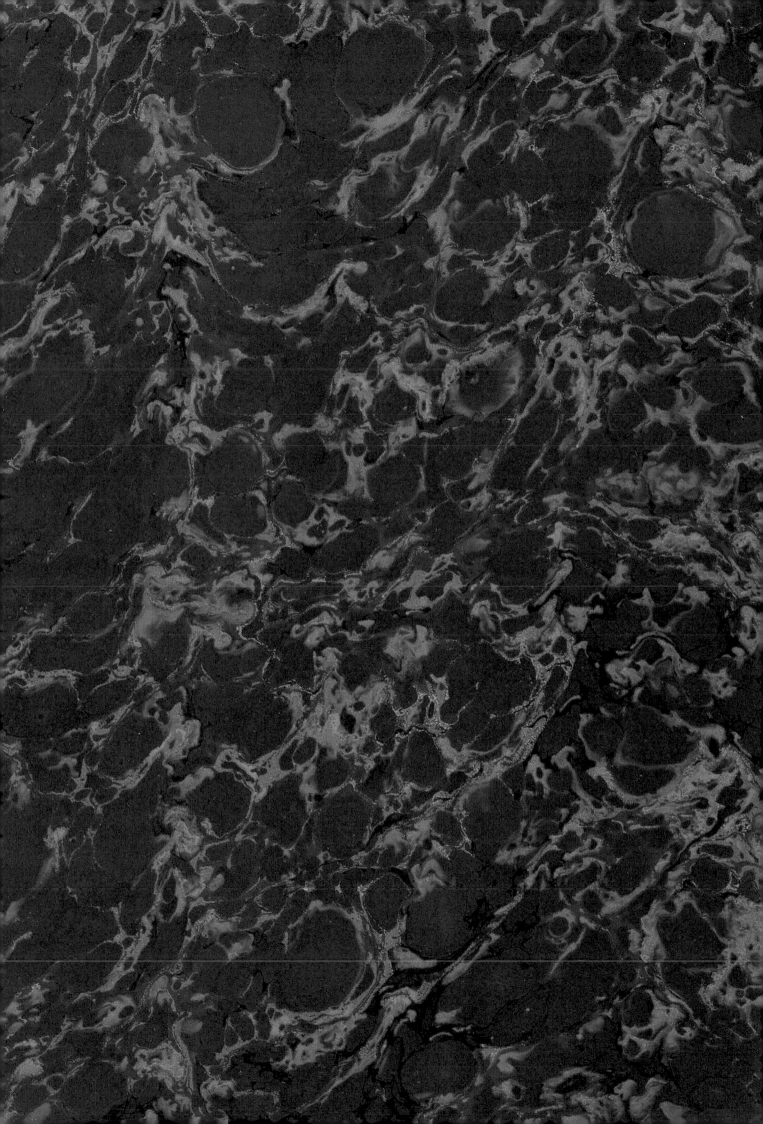

PART TWO

ON FILM

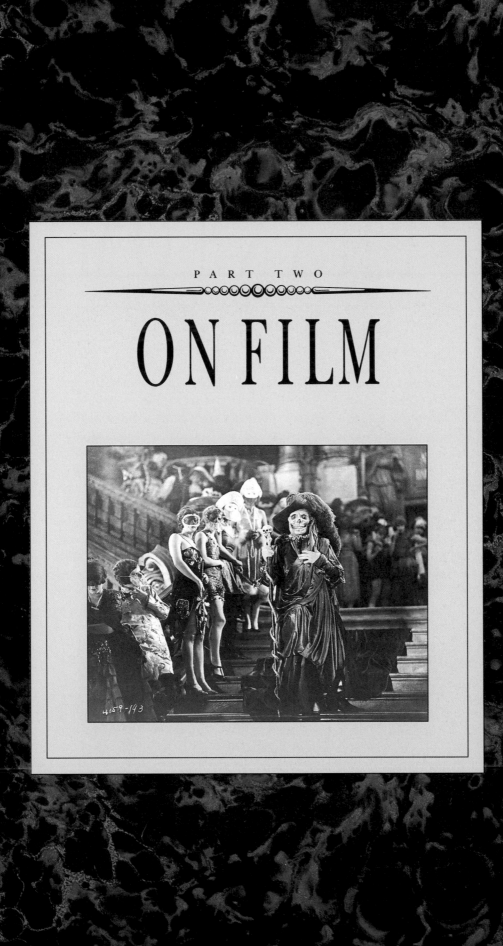

LON CHANEY'S
PHANTOM

*I*N THE summer of 1922 'Uncle' Carl Laemmle, the genial, tiny
president of Universal Pictures, took a vacation in Europe. He
was flush with success and in the ascendant as a movie mogul.
The tenth of thirteen children born to a Jewish family in Laupheim,
Germany, he had emigrated with them to the United States in 1884.
Carl, after working his way through the clothing business, had gone
into nickelodeons, or slot machine movie shows, in 1906. He had then
defied the notorious Motion Pictures Patents Company by setting up
a film-making firm, Independent Motion Pictures, or IMP, that
refused to pay them royalties. He could lay claim to having invented
the star system when he lured the unnamed 'Biograph girl' to his
company as Florence Lawrence, the IMP girl. It was he who
promoted Mary Pickford as 'The World's Sweetheart'. In 1915,
having seen the Patents Company into the ground, he opened
Universal City, a 230-acre studio lot near the obscure village of
Lankershim in the San Fernando Valley, and gave jobs to almost
everyone lucky enough to be a member of his huge family. (There was
a popular rhyme: 'Uncle Carl Laemmle, had a very large family'.)

In Paris Laemmle met Leroux, as one film man to another, and
confessed to him how excited he had been gazing at Garnier's opera
house from the Place de l'Opéra. Leroux, sensing some interest, gave
Laemmle a copy of *The Phantom of the Opera* for his bedtime reading.
Apparently that night Laemmle stayed awake, intent on getting
through the entire story. By the next morning he had determined that
it should be made into a film, but one that could be shot back home in
the Universal Studios rather than in Paris. In those days it was
cheaper to build a replica of the Paris Opéra on a stage in a
Californian film studio than to send a cast and crew to Europe. In any
case, his company was already committed to another Paris story, *The
Hunchback of Notre Dame*, and a huge outdoor set which included a
monstrous replica of the cathedral was in the process of erection on
the backlot.

The star of that film, playing the misshapen Quasimodo, was Lon
Chaney, whose ability to undergo fearsome physical deformation in
the assumption of his roles had already earned him a legendary
reputation. He was a master of make-up, 'the man of a thousand
faces', and although his appearances were frequently grotesque he
was able to project a degree of pathos sufficient to win the sympathy
of his audiences. To play the hunchback he wore on his back a rubber
hump that weighed forty pounds, and twisted his body with a

CARL LAEMMLE presents
"The Phantom of the Opera"

with
LON CHANEY
MARY PHILBIN
NORMAN KERRY
A. GIBSON GOWLAND
EDWIN CAREWE
and 5000 others
From the novel by
GASTON LEROUX
Directed by
RUPERT JULIAN

UNIVERSAL'S MASTERPIECE

The first and greatest 'Phantom' – a 1925 lobby card for the Lon Chaney film.

fearsome leather harness that weighed another thirty pounds. Such was his dedication that box-office success was assured, and Laemmle found his star being lured away by Metro-Goldwyn-Mayer.

In his view Chaney was the only actor who could ensure the success of the Phantom project, and he was obliged to enter into expensive negotiations with MGM to acquire his services. The MGM president, his deadly rival Louis B. Mayer, at first was reluctant to loan Chaney at all, but eventually agreed after an intervention by his young associate Irving Thalberg, who had cut his teeth as a producer at Universal. Thalberg argued that the Phantom could be the most significant role of Chaney's career, an instance of the prescience that had led him to being regarded as Hollywood's boy wonder. Chaney, too, was delighted to find himself back at his old studio for a much higher salary.

Meanwhile, it was decided that the principal set of the film was to be the opera house itself, and the building of the replica was begun on Stage 28 at the Universal studios. Because the auditorium would have five tiers of boxes, to be crammed with hundreds of extras, it was decided that the customary methods of set construction on a wooden framework would be inadequate and unsafe. Accordingly, it was the first Hollywood set to be based on a steel framework implanted in

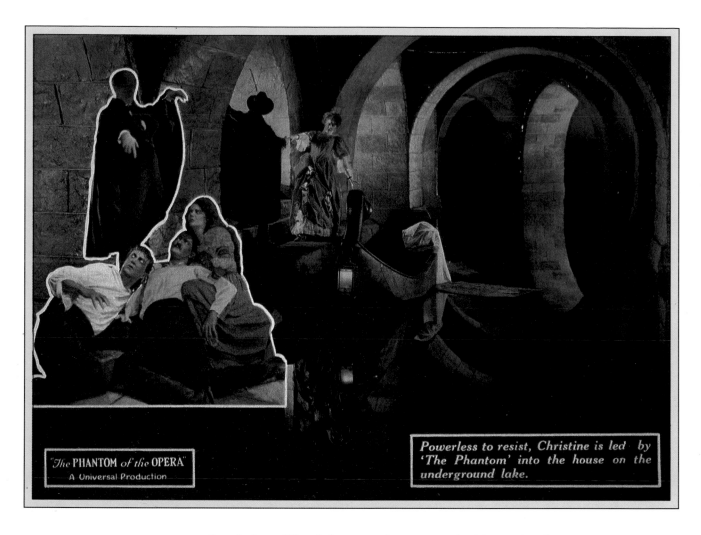

"The PHANTOM of the OPERA"
A Universal Production

Powerless to resist, Christine is led by 'The Phantom' into the house on the underground lake.

Bart Carre designed the subterranean setting: the Chaney lair beneath the Opéra.

concrete foundations. The skeleton was later covered with wood and reinforced corrugated iron.

So soundly was this huge indoor set built that it has never been struck. It still stands on Stage 28 to this day, and has appeared in many films over the years whenever a large auditorium is required, including the 1943 version of *The Phantom of the Opera*, several Deanna Durbin pictures, Ronald Colman's Academy award-winning *A Double Life* in 1948, Alfred Hitchcock's *Torn Curtain* in 1966, and *The Sting*, with Robert Redford, in 1973. The famous Universal City Tour, which is one of the largest tourist attractions in the western United States, includes Stage 28 on the itinerary, and it is visited by many thousands of sightseers every year. For that reason alone there has been a justification in keeping it standing, and it survives, a link with the old silent Hollywood of more than sixty years ago.

A tank had been built under the floor of the stage in order that the lake scenes and the Phantom's lair could be filmed. The backstage part of the set was fitted out so comprehensively that all the necessary equipment, scenery and props for the staging of a real opera were present. The roof, including the huge statue of Apollo, was built to full scale, and the Paris skyline was added with a glass painting mounted in front of the camera. Another spectacular area of the set was the Grand Foyer with the double staircase, a perfect setting for the masked ball, one of the most spectacular sequences in the film.

"The PHANTOM of the OPERA"
A Universal Production

"Back -- quick -- here he comes!"

Shooting began in the latter half of 1924. The director was Rupert Julian, a New Zealander who had emigrated to America in 1913. Initially an actor, he had soon turned to direction, and was responsible for a number of pot-boilers of little distinction. Then he was asked by Thalberg to replace Erich Von Stroheim, completing his 1923 film *The Merry-go-round* which had run into budgetary difficulties. Julian later claimed that only a fraction of the film's footage was Stroheim's, but clearly the look and shape of the film belonged to his predecessor. There was an affinity of manner with the extravagant Stroheim, and Julian was noted for his arrogant attitude on the set.

Not surprisingly in view of the fact that Chaney was also a difficult man to work with, a perfectionist with unshakeable views, the shooting of the film did not proceed either smoothly or harmoniously. For much of the time intermediaries had to negotiate between star and director, who were scarcely on speaking terms. The part of the young singer with whom Erik, the Phantom, is obsessed, was taken by Mary Philbin, a 21-year-old former beauty queen who had been given a chance by Erich Von Stroheim in *The Merry-go-round*. *The Phantom of the Opera* was her most notable film, and her career ended with the arrival of talking pictures. Norman Kerry played Raoul de Chagny, with John Sainpolis as his brother Philippe and Arthur Edmund Carewe as a mysterious character, Ledoux, who replaces Leroux's Persian.

Ten weeks after filming had started, a rough assembly of the

Arthur Edmund Carewe (Ledoux) shows Norman Kerry (Raoul) how to fend off the Punjab lasso.

footage was shown to the studio hierarchy led by Laemmle, who found the pace too slow. As a consequence of the showing and the history of problems with Chaney, Laemmle ordered that Rupert Julian be replaced by Edward Sedgwick, an action and comedy director. It was he who shot the mob and chase scenes at the climax of the film. Then, following Los Angeles previews in January 1925, Sedgwick was asked to add a new subplot. The premiere was in San Francisco on 26 April 1925, and even after it had taken place it was decided to withdraw the print, remove the additional material and instead to intersperse a few comic moments, using the Mack Sennett comedian Chester Conklin as a portly stagehand. When the new print was shipped to New York the East Coast backers viewed it with stupefaction, finding that the storyline made little sense. So now the comedy was excised, the whole film re-edited and a new set of title cards was hastily prepared to cover the strange editing shifts. The 1925 release prints showed signs of the massive tinkering the film had undergone. Some sequences, such as the opening ballet and the masked ball, were shot in the old two-colour Technicolor process which required greatly enhanced lighting, but the rest of the film was in black-and-white with occasional use of tinted stock for the release prints, a common practice at the time.

Chaney disguised as Red Death makes his nightmarish entrance to the masked ball.

Given such a chequered production history it is surprising that the film could have turned out so well. That it did, and became a major box-office hit of the year in America, was largely on the strength of Chaney's performance which overcame the glaring continuity lapses. Chaney had astutely arranged for a contractual clause prohibiting the use of any photographs of his Phantom make-up before the film was released, a suggestion with which the studio concurred. He had resolved to make it a *tour de force* that would strike terror throughout the audience, and he succeeded. There is a classic moment in the film when Mary Philbin snatches his mask off from behind. The revelation as Chaney faces the camera with his horrific countenance exposed, and then turns to confront Philbin, who is overcome with terror, sent such shudders through the audience that theatre managers were urged by the distributors' publicists to lay in stocks of smelling salts for nervous ladies who were likely to faint at the awful sight.

The Opéra auditorium set, designed by Charles Hall, still standing at Universal City.

Contrary to popular belief, Chaney's make-up was not based on a mask, but on his real face. He inserted a wire device into his nose to push his nostrils apart and give it an upturned look. He placed celluloid discs inside his cheeks to change the facial shape. Drops in his eyes produced the bulging pop-eyed look. The result was one of the greatest contributions to the iconography of the silent cinema. Typically, Chaney set himself a task that would have daunted most actors – and succeeded, for in spite of a macabre and repulsive appearance he was able to project so much compassion and sorrow that it was perfectly possible to feel sympathy for this misshapen creature. Chaney's parents had been deaf mutes, and from his earliest childhood he had been obliged to signify his feelings through expression and gesture, which was a contributing factor to his success as a silent star. He only made one talking picture before his death from bronchial cancer in 1930.

But Chaney's Phantom look was also a hard one to imitate. James

Lon Chaney's horrific, disfiguring make-up that caused ladies to call for the smelling salts.

Cagney came nowhere near it when he played Chaney in the 1957 film biography *Man of a Thousand Faces*, another film which used the opera house set on Stage 28.

The set designs of the 1925 film were especially memorable. Most of them were the work of Charles D. Hall, but Bart Carre designed the subterranean sets, including the Phantom's lair, with his bed in the form of a coffin and Christine's bed shaped like a boat. The descent of the chandelier was achieved by lowering it slowly on a rope while an undercranked camera focused on it. When the film was played at normal speed it appeared to drop at a hideously lethal rate.

Erik the Phantom was not given the background that Leroux had worked out for him. Instead he was an escapee from Devil's Island who had been confined during the Commune in a dungeon and torture chamber under the Opéra. Ten years later he is still living out of sight in the depths and falls in love with Christine Daaé, becoming her secret music master who talks to her from behind the wall in her dressing-room. To boost her career he terrorizes the opera house, and lures Christine to his home across the subterranean lake. He is able to foil pursuers by swimming under water, drawing breath through a bamboo tube. Christine is faced with a dilemma: by turning either an ornamental grasshopper or scorpion she could blow the building sky high or save Raoul. In trying to come to her rescue, he has fallen into an old torture chamber with the secret policeman, Ledoux, who is also on the Phantom's trail. She chooses correctly, and the men are able to save her. The Phantom, however, kidnaps her again and makes off in a carriage through the streets of Paris into the night. Then Christine falls out, and is once again reunited with Raoul. Meanwhile the Phantom crashes, and the vengeful mob in pursuit capture him and club him to death, throwing the body into the Seine.

The American success of the film was not echoed in Great Britain, where a publicity stunt misfired. The British newspapers had been reporting on extraordinary scenes of horror-stricken audiences in the United States, who had been lining up and paying their money at the box office to be shocked to the core. Consequently there was already a considerable degree of interest before a print had even reached British shores. An over-keen publicist for the European Motion Picture Company, the importers, arranged for a contingent of soldiers to escort the first print from Southampton Docks to London, in order to draw attention to the precious nature of the cargo. The public, led by those who write letters to *The Times*, was so incensed by this scandalous misuse of a detachment of the British army that the Cinematograph Exhibitors' Association was prevailed upon to ban the film in the name of patriotism and the British Empire. The ban was only lifted some years later, in November 1928, when Laemmle himself made a personal plea to the exhibitors. By then the Phantom had gone off the boil.

The Julian film took fewer liberties with Leroux's story than subsequent versions. A scene at the beginning, where the ballet girls are skittering about backstage, twirling and shrieking in excitement as they relish the frissons of fear that the Phantom, as yet merely a shadow on the wall, is giving them, is an effective and slightly erotic

James Cagney plays Chaney in 'Man of a Thousand Faces'.

Cagney imitated Chaney's stance in the 1957 film biography.

interpretation of Leroux's first chapter. But the acting, lighting and staging of the film as a whole are old-fashioned for their time. By the mid-1920s the silent cinema had learned to curb the excessively theatrical gestures of the early days and rely more on subtlety of facial expression. But *The Phantom of the Opera* has the old histrionics in abundance, with Mary Philbin, the frizzy-haired heroine, clapping her hand to her brow, wringing her hands and shrinking in terror like a barnstorming actress in a transpontine melodrama. It is the director who is largely responsible for her excesses, since she is effective enough when she is still, as, for instance, in her trance-like state as she hears the Phantom's voice in her dressing-room. But in the panic after the chandelier has fallen on the audience she stands out in a crowd shot in which everyone is rushing forwards – she is the only one who is walking out of the shot backwards.

To share scenes with Lon Chaney could not have been an easy task for anyone, since he was one of a handful of film performers with sufficient magnetism to compel an audience's attention no matter what was happening elsewhere in the scene. His entrance is cleverly delayed, heightening the anticipation. In the first reels his presence is established merely as a shadow against a wall or a mysterious silhouette glimpsed for a second in Box 5. But later appearances are calculated to exert the maximum fascination. There is the first descent with Christine into the cellars, where she is led by him downwards through a series of interconnecting ramps on horseback, then poled across the Stygian black lake. There is the shock effect of the Phantom's entrance on the crowded Grand Staircase at the masked ball, the dancers parting like the Red Sea before Moses as he parades in the fiendish costume of Red Death, in velvet breeches, a cloak and a feathered, broad-brimmed hat, contemplating the scene

*R*aoul and Christine: a lobby card.

*R*ed Death overhears the lovers at the ball. The Phantom and his protégée in his secret home (opposite).

through a death's head mask (allegedly Chaney's own face grotesquely made-up) and holding a long cane with a skull for a handle. Later, as Raoul and Christine retreat to the opera house roof in the belief that they are out of earshot of the Phantom his cloak is first glimpsed above them, like a silk flag billowing in the night wind from the Apollo statue, before he is revealed suffering in anguish from Christine's betrayal.

The secret policeman, Ledoux, is always seen in evening clothes and an incongruous astrakhan cap ('The Persian'), suspected by some of being the Phantom himself, since he seems never far away from the last manifestation. When Raoul and Christine return from the roof to the revelry of the masked ball, he points them in a safe direction. Later he reveals that he has kept the Phantom under observation for many months, but not long enough to avert the chandelier tragedy which must have cost several lives in the audience. He leads Raoul down into the basements, showing how holding one hand level with the head can counter the effect of the deadly Punjab lasso, the weapon used by the Phantom to despatch Buquet, the stagehand, who knew too much. When the men are trapped in the torture chamber it turns out to be a mirrored room ornamented with cardboard palm trees, scarcely the stereotype for such places, but the relevance of the bogus tropicality becomes plain when Erik unleashes a massive amount of searing heat which turns the room into an oven and threatens to roast its gasping occupants.

The flight from the pursuing mob, shot by Edward Sedgwick, while very dramatic, is not part of Leroux's narrative. It could cynically be suggested that it presented an opportunity to make use of the left-over sets from *The Hunchback of Notre Dame*, and since it takes place by night the medieval character of the architecture is less apparent, except for one superb camera angle which embraces the intricate west front of Nôtre Dame itself. The fury of the mob as they fall on Erik and hack him to death is both callous and gruesome, and the film ends somewhat abruptly with his corpse disappearing into the murky waters, with the word 'Finis' superimposed as soon as they have closed on the remains.

Two years after *The Phantom of the Opera* was released, Warner Brothers brought out *The Jazz Singer*, and started the talking picture revolution. The silent picture was doomed, and studios not only hastened the transition to sound, but looked closely at their existing product to determine whether or not it was suitable for adaptation to the new medium of talkies. In 1930 dialogue sequences were shot for *The Phantom of the Opera* with Mary Philbin and Norman Kerry, and music and sound effects were added to the whole film. Some sections were eliminated altogether, while singing voices were added to the various scenes from *Faust* that were incorporated in the action. Mary Philbin's singing was dubbed none too satisfactorily, as the technique was then in its infancy. Lon Chaney's voice was purported to be heard, but actually dubbed by someone else, since he was not involved in the sound version, and died in the same year. Although only a third of the film had dialogue and singing, it was advertised with the line 'Talking! Singing! Dancing! Sound Effects! Music! Color!' And so the first Phantom on film enjoyed a renewed lease of life.

OTHER
VISIONS

WHEN inspiration flags, Hollywood has always had the habit of reaching back into the locker and resurrecting a triumph from the past. Remakes of past hits are commonplace; the number that prove to be better in quality than the original could probably be counted on one hand. Universal's successful silent movie *The Phantom of the Opera* had its turn in 1943. By the early Forties the studio had become undistinguished in comparison with its more glamorous rivals such as MGM, Paramount and Warner. Universal was the home of Deanna Durbin musicals, Abbott and Costello comedies and a successful series of Sherlock Holmes thrillers featuring Basil Rathbone and Nigel Bruce. But most of the studio's output was destined for the lower half of the double bills then customary in cinema programming.

However, the new Phantom film was to be different. It was conceived on a more lavish scale than was the norm during the economy-conscious climate prevailing in the middle of the Second World War. It was to be made in glorious Technicolor with a budget of $1.75 million, a considerable sum for the time. The money, however, was mainly spent on a large cast of singers, lavish costumes and a great many musical sequences. So it was the opera, rather than the Phantom, that won in the end. Originally it had been intended that it should be a musical extravaganza, a vehicle for the popular young singing star Deanna Durbin in the role of Christine, to be directed by Henry Koster, with Broderick Crawford as the Phantom. Following the United States' entry into the Second World War in December 1941 Crawford was drafted into military service. The next choice for the part was the portly Charles Laughton, a celebrated British character actor of immaculate diction who had lately scored a success in the studio's remake of *The Hunchback of Notre Dame* directed by William Diertele in 1940. There was a delay in getting things moving on the new film, and the original team broke up.

By 1943 it had been decided that the new version of *The Phantom of the Opera* should be a vehicle for the popular movieland tenor, Nelson Eddy, teaming him with a newish singer, Susanna Foster, who had made her début in *The Great Victor Herbert* in 1940 at the age of fifteen. Eddy's celebrated saccharine partnership with Jeanette MacDonald as 'America's singing sweethearts' had begun in 1933, but had terminated in 1942 with *I Married an Angel*, after which MGM had failed to renew MacDonald's contract. The new producer of *The Phantom of the Opera* at Universal, George Waggner, had hopes that

Eddy could ease his way into a new screen partnership with the teenage Foster. Arthur Lubin, a director of average ability on the Universal lot – his highspots hitherto had been Abbott and Costello comedies – was given the assignment, possibly because the draft board was removing many of the ablest young men. The resulting film, while unexceptional, was probably the best Lubin ever made.

Leroux's storyline was completely revised, and the names of many of the characters changed. Claude Rains, a soft-spoken and distinguished British actor, was cast as Erique Claudin, a shy, middle-aged violinist in the orchestra, who has been using his hard-won earnings to pay secretly for singing lessons for the diva's understudy, Christine Dubois, for whom he has an unrequited passion. She is not only unaware of how her tuition is financed but has two suitors, Anatole Garron, a tenor in the opera, played by Nelson Eddy, and Raoul De Chagny, a dashingly uniformed, St Cyr-trained inspector in the Sûreté, played by Edgar Barrier.

Claudin is a sad case. Fired from his orchestral job because his playing skills are fading, he attempts to sell his concerto to an unsympathetic publisher. Hearing one of his own compositions played in the next room, and believing that he has been robbed, he attacks the publisher, but a female assistant throws a tray full of etching acid in his face. He escapes from the police by hiding in the sewers.

Later the managers of the opera house discover that food, costumes and other items are being mysteriously spirited away, and there are backstage sightings of a mysterious cloaked figure. It is thought to be the Opéra ghost. Christine is addressed by a hidden voice, and the diva to whom she is understudy is murdered in her dressing-room. A note is received by the management urging that Christine sing the leading role in a new production, but in order to draw the Phantom into the open at Inspector De Chagny's request someone else is given the role. The angry Phantom cuts the chain that suspends the

Claude Rains wears the mask of the Phantom.

*T*he Phantom leads Christine (Susanna Foster) to his lair.

*B*ogus Opera: 'Le Prince de Caucasie', cobbled together from Tchaikovsky, with hero Nelson Eddy (left).

chandelier over the auditorium. In the hubbub following its lethal descent during a performance he abducts Christine from the back-stage area, taking her to his underground lair, where he plays his piano concerto to her. She is urged to sing and does so unwillingly. Raoul and Anatole are in pursuit through the cellars and hear her voice. Meanwhile she snatches the Phantom's mask and reveals the disfigured face of Claudin. At that moment her rescuers burst in, a shot is fired and Claudin is killed by a rock fall; the others run away to escape in the nick of time. Later the two rivals each invite Christine to supper after her triumph on the Opéra stage, but when she indicates that she is more interested in operatic fame than being partnered by either of them they go off together, two bachelors on the town.

It can be seen that the impact of Leroux's story has been hopelessly blunted by the writers (Eric Taylor and Samuel Hoffenstein, with adaptation by John Jacoby) in order to make the film more of a musical spectacular than a creepy and bizarre thriller. Gounod's *Faust*, which had been so important in the original story, was not used. Instead there were excerpts from Friedrich Von Flotow's *Martha* and two bogus operas concocted for the film, the first, *Amour et Gloire*, using themes from Chopin, and the other, *Le Prince de Caucasie*, based on Tchaikowsky's Symphony No 4. There was also a theme song, *Lullaby of the Bells*, by Edward Ward, the film's musical director, and George Waggner, the producer, which was also heard as a violin solo and as the Phantom's piano concerto.

There is also little of the terror of the 1925 film. Claudin's escape from the police after the acid throwing is handled very conventionally, with a convenient manhole cover located beneath a stationary carriage offering the means to safety, even if the officers stand on the grating a few seconds after the fugitive, his flesh melting from the corrosive effects of the acid, has closed it over his head. The shots of the falling chandelier are almost exact replications of the 1925 film, using an under-cranked camera. Even the revelation of Claude Rains' face after his mask has been snatched off is unspectacular when compared with Chaney's make-up. Here it looks nothing worse than an unpleasant skin ailment.

In spite of a lack of enthusiasm from the critics, who were not prepared to compare it favourably with the Lon Chaney film, the public appeared to like it. It was certainly a luxurious production. At the time it was made there was a strictly enforced budgetary ceiling imposed on set construction, amounting to a mere $10,000 for most films. It called for ingenuity on the part of the designers in utilizing existing material, which is one of the reasons why many Hollywood films of the Forties appear to be borrowing each other's sets. *The Phantom of the Opera* had a head start in that the sumptuous opera house set on Stage 28 was there already, and only needed minor refurbishment to bring it up to the requirements of Technicolor. The Phantom's lair was more difficult, and is far less convincing, looking more like disused mine workings than an opera house basement. Although the lake is there, it is only skirted by the actors on foot. It was presumably impossible to rebuild the 1925 Grand Foyer set, and so the masked ball sequence does not exist in this version.

George Waggner was sufficiently excited by the public response to use a similar theme for *The Climax*, which he also directed, with Boris Karloff believing that Susanna Foster is the reincarnation of the prima donna murdered by him a decade previously, and embalmed in a vault beneath the auditorium. Although it presented a further opportunity to use the opera house set, it was less successful than its predecessor.

When James Cagney played Lon Chaney in *Man of a Thousand Faces* in 1957, the Phantom briefly strode at Universal again, with the opera house set being called upon for a sequence representing the making of the 1925 film. But although Cagney was careful to eschew his familiar mannerisms to play the role, he was badly let down by a maudlin script.

In 1962 *The Phantom of the Opera* was filmed once more, but this time in London by Hammer Films, who had gained a reputation for their cheaply made horror films. The director was Terence Fisher, and the Phantom was played by Herbert Lom, with Heather Sears as his victim. It was more a remake of the 1943 version than a recapitulation of the 1925 film, but there was a significant difference in that the Phantom was now a wholly sympathetic character, blamed for the foul deeds of a new menace, the Dwarf, and he dies attempting to save the heroine from the falling chandelier.

Curiously, the film lacks even the tension of the 1943 version as a consequence, and it received poor critical notices. Again *Faust* was dropped from the story, this time in favour of an original composition by Edward Astley, an opera based on a St Joan theme. The setting was also now Victorian England, with London a city of gaslight and cobbles. The mythical London Opera House was in fact Wimbledon Theatre, in south-west London. This magnificently exuberant building has frequently earned its precarious keep as a working theatre by having its auditorium rented out as a location for film and television companies.

It was also the theatre in which the Actors' Company presented a stage version, much more faithful to Leroux, in June 1975. This production, with Sharon Duce as Christine, Keith Drinkel as Raoul and Edward Petherbridge as Erik, was adapted and directed by David Giles.

There have been other films based on *The Phantom of the Opera*. In 1960, in Mexico, Fernando Cortes directed *El Fantasma de la Opereta*, a comic version with the knockabout comedian Tin-Tan. The film was essentially a cheaply made parody and seems to have vanished.

In 1974 a television movie, *Phantom of Hollywood*, was made, directed by Gene Levitt, which took as its setting not an opera house, but a movie studio. The Phantom was an old, disfigured actor, played by Jack Cassidy, who had hidden out on the lot for thirty years, but when the bulldozers come to destroy his home he goes on a wild rampage. A witty idea, but somewhat deflated by the inadequate script. It seems to have been dreamed up largely to find dramatic possibilities in the carve-up and destruction of sets on the huge MGM backlot at Culver City which was going on at the time. Several old Hollywood names also appear in it, including Broderick Crawford, Peter Lawford, Corinne Calvet, Jackie Coogan and John Ireland.

Herbert Lom as the Phantom in the Hammer version of the legend.

*Lom unmasked in the
1962 film, directed by
Terence Fisher.*

A television movie nearer to the Universal *Phantom*, but so far
removed from Leroux that his name did not even appear on the
credits, was broadcast in the United States by CBS in January 1983.
The setting this time was Hungary, where filming had taken place,
using a convenient warren of tunnels under a brewery. The opera
house scenes were filmed in the theatre at Kecskemet, as the Budapest
Opera House was not available. The Phantom was played by
Maximilian Schell, with Jane Seymour as his victim and Michael
York as her lover. Others in the cast included Jeremy Kemp, Philip
Stone and Diana Quick. The director was Robert Markowitz and the
screenwriter Sherman Yellen.

The setting is Budapest before the First World War. The wife of the
conductor makes her début, but a powerful impresario and spurned
lover organizes a bad notice. She kills herself and her husband, in a
struggle with the critic responsible, knocks over a heater setting his
clothes alight. He douses himself with what he thinks is water but is
really acid. Permanently scarred he crawls off to the sewers to don the
phantom mask. Later a young singer seems to resemble his dead wife,
which is hardly surprising since she is played by the same actress. The
Phantom then sets out on his terrifying plan to destroy his enemies
and make sure that the girl has the success denied his wife.

A more interesting film variant was Brian De Palma's rock version,
The Phantom of the Paradise, in 1974. Paul Williams, who composed
most of the music, also appeared as Swan, a Machiavellian record
impresario, with William Finley as Winslow Leach, an unknown

composer whose music on a Faust theme he steals for his new rock palace, the Paradise. Winslow is framed and sent to Sing Sing. He escapes, breaks into Swan's record factory to do some sabotage, but gets his head stuck in a disc-pressing machine. He adopts a birdlike mask to hide his deformity together with a long cape and haunts the Paradise more or less openly until persuaded by Swan to complete his rock opera on the Faust legend. Winslow agrees providing that Phoenix, a girl singer (Jessica Harper) by whom he is infatuated, has the lead. Swan secretly assigns Beef (Gerrit Graham), a gay musclebound male, in the part, but the Phantom kills him. Then Winslow discovers that Swan has signed a pact with the Devil and is planning to have Phoenix assassinated on coast-to-coast television. In the final confrontation with Swan the TV rock fans of America see their spectacular deaths instead.

Thus two legends, that of Faust, and that of the Phantom of the Opera are fused in one work, not entirely satisfactorily. The film has enthusiasm but lacks coherence and sureness, being part pop-rock spectacle, part camp comic-strip send-up. It was not a success when first released, and attempts to re-market it with a different advertising strategy also failed. It did, however, establish a cult following, and has continued to enjoy late night campus screenings. Brian De Palma, a graduate of the underground school of film-making with a style based on parody and satire, went on to specialize in macabre thrillers such as *Carrie, Dressed to Kill* and *Body Double* with no mean success. One wonders what he would have achieved if had made a version of Leroux's *Phantom*.

It has to be noticed that all the films after Lon Chaney, whether directly based on the story, or merely using it as in the last case as a springboard, shy away from the premise that the Phantom, or Erik, was born deformed but was of high intelligence, rather like the Elephant Man, and that his psychological condition stemmed from his need to hide away from the real world and create an environment in which he can be the unchallenged master. Scriptwriters have found it easier to deal with a normal man suffering a wrong and an accidental disfigurement. Thus the Phantom's obsession has been simplified and coarsened, and his troglodyte existence rendered implausible (how does he in such a short space of time find and furnish his lair even to the extent of installing a piano?). Leroux gave his Phantom not only many years to establish himself but also an architectural training and oriental experience in building secret hideaways, as well as a contract from Garnier himself to work on the extended construction of the opera house. Leroux's Phantom did go out into the streets and ride in cabs, wearing a less frightening disguise than the mask used for his opera house terror, and was, in spite of this bizarre appearance, able to comport himself like other men.

Nevertheless, Gaston Leroux's yarn, written in the spirit of a pot-boiling sensational thriller, has survived these and other variations, plainly possessing the imaginative qualities that the public appreciate. It is, after all, a familiar love story, a version of the Beauty and the Beast. Every great opera house deserves its ghost, and Leroux obliged Paris by supplying one, providing a romantic legend that would assure its durability on film and in the theatre.

William Finley as Winslow Leach in 'The Phantom of the Paradise', a rock variation directed by Brian de Palma in 1974.

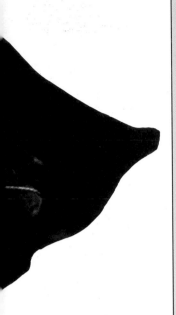

Jane Seymour and
Maximilian Schell (right),
in the 1982 version made
in Hungary for CBS
television.

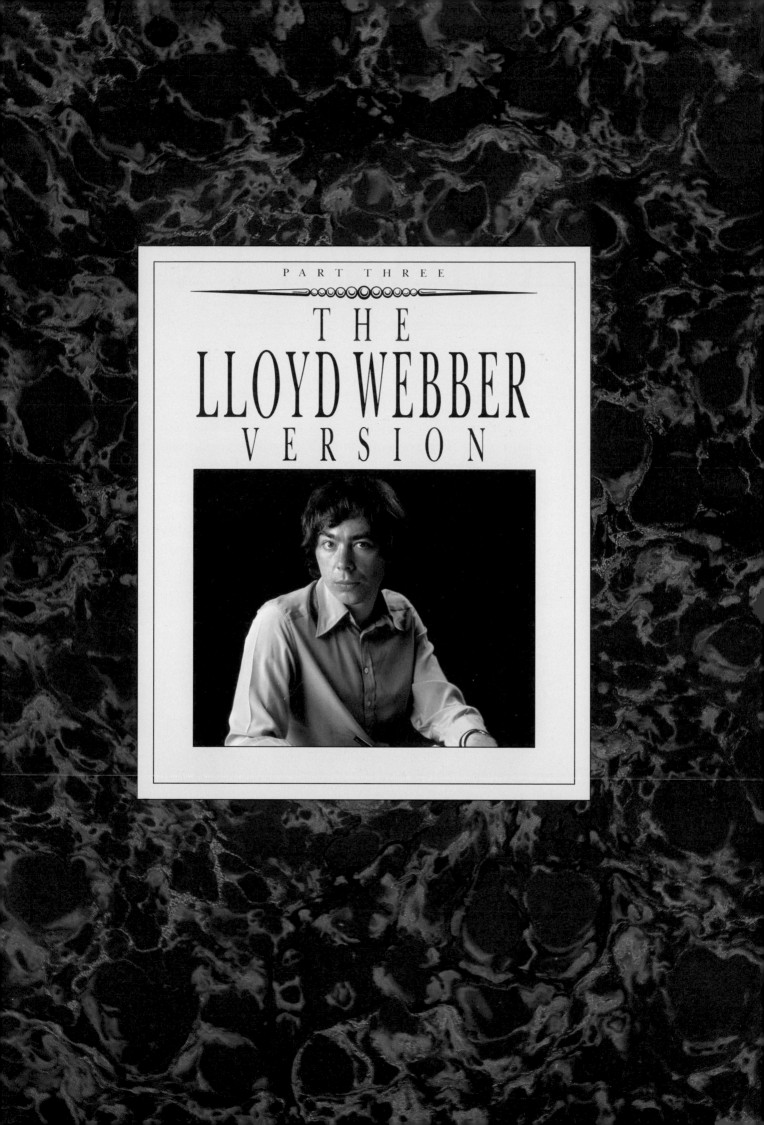

PART THREE

THE LLOYD WEBBER VERSION

THE PHANTOM
TRIUMPHANT

*C*ontrary to the general impression, it was not Andrew Lloyd Webber who was the first to turn Gaston Leroux's compelling story into a stage musical. There have been various attempts, particularly in the United States, and in 1984 a rumbustious and unashamedly camp version of *The Phantom of the Opera* was mounted at the Theatre Royal, Stratford, in East London, using generous portions of the music of Verdi, Gounod and Offenbach, and a dash of Grand Guignol to set the mood. The director, Ken Hill, approached the 23-year-old singer-dancer, Sarah Brightman, shortly to become the second Mrs Andrew Lloyd Webber, to play Christine. This was largely on the strength of her performance in the Charles Strouse opera for children, *Nightingale*, but she had to decline because of her other commitments.

Prompted by a review of Ken Hill's version in the *Daily Telegraph*, Lloyd Webber contacted Cameron Mackintosh, producer of many successful shows of the Eighties both in the West End and on Broadway, and who had co-presented Lloyd Webber's own *Cats* and *Song and Dance*. 'It was one day in the spring of 1984 – I was lying in the bath when Andrew rang,' said Mackintosh. 'His first words were: "If I said to you *Phantom of the Opera*, what would you say?" I remembering answering, "I think it's a good idea."'

Mackintosh arranged a screening of the Lon Chaney film of 1925, which they found evocative, in spite of its intrinsic flaws. They also went to see Ken Hill's production which they thought could be developed into a West End success which they would produce using real opera. Ken Hill was commissioned to do a new treatment. 'There was no question of my composing the score,' said Lloyd Webber. 'We had something like *The Rocky Horror Show* in mind.'

The high-camp cult musical of the Seventies had been directed by Jim Sharman, who had also staged *Jesus Christ Superstar*, the first West End success of Andrew Lloyd Webber and the lyricist Tim Rice. While Mackintosh and Lloyd Webber were in Tokyo later in 1984 for the Japanese opening of *Cats*, they saw Sharman and tried to secure his interest in their idea for a *Phantom* romp, with *Raiders of the Lost Ark*-type chases through the underground labyrinth, the show taking place against a score arranged from contemporary works by Delibes, Massenet and Gounod.

However, Sharman had become primarily a director of mainstream opera and legit theatre in his native Australia, and had to tell Mackintosh and Lloyd Webber that he was not available. 'But also,'

he added, 'you're missing a great romantic plot – you should compose the score.'

Nine months later, browsing in a secondhand bookstore in New York, Lloyd Webber came across a faded copy of the original novel, which was not only out of print but also out of copyright, for a dollar. Mackintosh discovered another tucked away in a pile of books belonging to his aunt.

Lloyd Webber's attitude to the material was transformed. He was especially impressed that in the novel Christine keeps her promise to return to the Phantom, at his death, the ring he entrusted to her. He also enjoyed the little touches of humour Leroux endowed to his Phantom – a humour the music deliberately reflects in the shock horror chords of the title theme. Another aspect of the Phantom which amused Lloyd Webber was the fact that he had an excellent wine cellar.

'I was actually writing something else at the time, one of the earliest treatments of my 1989 musical, David Garnett's *Aspects of Love,'* said Lloyd Webber, 'and I realized that the reason I was hung up was because what I was trying to write was a major romantic story, and I had been trying to do that ever since I started my career, but I had never been able to find the plot that could be my – er – as it were – *South Pacific.* Then, with the Phantom, it was there! I called Cameron and

Sarah Brightman and Steve Harley (top), *from the promotional video for 'The Phantom of the Opera'; Sarah Brightman and Cliff Richard* (middle), *from the video 'All I Ask of You'; Michael Crawford* (bottom), *from the video 'Music of the Night'.*

said, "I think if I follow the romance in the novel it could be the plot I'm looking for – I'll give it a go."'

Next to come into Lloyd Webber's sights was the director. Hal Prince, who since the Fifties has directed or produced many legendary musicals, including *The Pajama Game, West Side Story, Fiddler on the Roof, Cabaret* and the Rice–Lloyd Webber collaboration, *Evita*, met with him in New York. 'Hal told me that what he wanted to do was a great romantic musical. I said, "What do you think about *Phantom of the Opera?*" He said, "It sounds terrific, what have you done?" I said, "I haven't really done anything yet, but come and see me in England."'

Each summer Andrew Lloyd Webber mounts an intimate music festival in his country home at Sydmonton. Performances there of embryonic works have helped shape their subsequent direction. In July 1985 the first act of *The Phantom of the Opera* was presented to the invited audience in its early draft form. The lyrics were written by Richard Stilgoe, an accomplished writer and musician who had provided the words for Lloyd Webber's noisy 1984 hit, *Starlight Express*. It was decided to build real sets for the mini-theatre, which is an ancient, tiny church in the grounds of the Lloyd Webber estate. Cameron Mackintosh and Lloyd Webber had both been impressed by the work of the stage designer Maria Björnson for the English National Opera and the Royal Shakespeare Company, particularly the imaginative manner in which she used the texture and weight of drapes to create an emotionally charged atmosphere. At that time she had never worked in the mainstream commercial theatre. Striking in appearance, and a fierce whirlwind of energy, she appears to live only for her work, often toiling long into the early morning hours in her basement studio in London.

The cast at Sydmonton was largely that already committed to the imminent Cameron Mackintosh/RSC production of *Les Misérables*, with Colm Wilkinson singing the part of the Phantom. Sarah Brightman played Christine, a role that Andrew Lloyd Webber was shaping for her, skilfully creating sweeping melodies to exercise her wonderfully pure voice.

Sydmonton, albeit only a taster for the show to come, was a spectacular success, with the resourceful Maria Björnson even contriving a chandelier to fall over the audience. 'It worked, it really worked,' said Mackintosh of the occasion.

Nevertheless, there followed a period of intense discussions. Andrew Lloyd Webber remained certain that Hal Prince was the right director. He had already played him the music privately before the Sydmonton performance, which Prince had deliberately not attended.

Said Lloyd Webber: 'The festival revealed that it was potentially a great romantic musical, and that a campy approach would be counter-productive to the whole thing. It was right to go with Hal because a romantic musical was what he really wanted to do, and his experience as an opera director for several years meant that he understood clearly every resonance that we were talking about. I have never dug my toes in so firmly anywhere as I did over *Phantom* – it had to be Hal.'

Hal Prince was equally certain. 'I said "Yes" immediately. I don't usually say "yes" right away. It was exactly the sort of show I wanted to do – I felt that there was a real need for a romantic show. I had done several that were hard-edged and bitter, even *Evita* is like that. I wanted a change as much for the theatre-goer as the director.'

Prince made a pilgrimage to the Paris Opéra and spent many hours climbing over every inch of the building from the subterranean lake to the topmost pinnacle, where he ventured along narrow catwalks unsupported by handrails and found himself looking down on the roof of the Galeries Lafayette, the great department store. Maria Björnson and her assistant carried out a similar reconnaissance, made even more hazardous by their constant taking of hundreds of Polaroids that would serve her as reference when it came to the set design.

As with earlier shows, Lloyd Webber decided in the spring of 1985 to test the water with a record which would encapsulate the story as he then saw it. A stylish and extravagant video accompanied the single, directed by Ken Russell with all his visually flamboyant skill, in which Steve Harley, the former lead singer of the rock group Cockney Rebel, played the Phantom. The tune, 'The Phantom of the Opera', was arranged as a rock number, the lyrics were specially written, and the single reached No. 7 in the charts.

Now that Andrew Lloyd Webber was hard at work composing the music for the rest of the show and determining the final shape that it would take, there were other important and possibly brutal creative decisions that had to be made. 'Richard Stilgoe is a good lyricist, and knows a lot about opera, but I believed that he would not be able to do it on his own. Romance is a tightrope, and it's very hard to write. It was something that in the end was my own decision, because as a composer you must get the libretto you want,' said Lloyd Webber.

An old friend and a giant of the musical theatre, Alan Jay Lerner, was approached for help in untangling the story. Lloyd Webber recalled Lerner's reaction: 'He said, "Dear boy, its your best score so far. You're not in as bad trouble as you think. The main thing you must not do with this plot is to ask too many questions – because it works!" But three weeks later he wrote to me to say that although he would love to do it more than anything, he was too ill.' The great lyricist of *Brigadoon* and *My Fair Lady*, *Gigi* and *Camelot* was shortly to die of cancer.

Lloyd Webber's friend and collaborator on *Evita*, Tim Rice, was also asked, but at the time his life was dominated by his new show, *Chess*, scheduled to open in May 1986.

The lyricist eventually chosen was an unknown, found in a musical writers' competition, which, as he later pointed out, he did not even win. Charles Hart was twenty-five and inexperienced, but had a good musical ear, and the facility to set poignant and appropriate words to the Lloyd Webber melodies. He was recruited after he had written some lyrics to a tape sent to him by Andrew Lloyd Webber without realizing that they were for *Phantom*, and modestly assumed that he was offered the job because he had the same kind of typewriter as Tim Rice.

In spite of his late arrival to the project he immediately accepted the deep romanticism of the story and the special potency of the situation in which a talented young woman is in thrall to three male

*H*al Prince directs.

*C*harles Hart.

figures – her high-born lover, her deceased father and Erik, the Phantom. He worked against the clock to keep up with the flow of Lloyd Webber's music, but his own musical knowledge proved invaluable, allowing the two to communicate in the special shorthand of musicians. The lyrics were produced in three months.

Although the new version of *Phantom* was to be closer to the Leroux story than any of the films, it was considerably adapted to heighten its dramatic effect in the theatre. Lloyd Webber believes that the construction of a musical is one of the most important ingredients in its success. 'Clearly, one of the biggest problems was the unmasking of the Phantom. In the cinema tremendous impact can be made by virtue of a close-up shot, but we had to devise a way that would make the unmasking effective from any point in a big musical theatre. I therefore decided we had to move the moment of the unmasking to a situation where a large number of characters could react to it rather than only Christine as was written in the book. The book gave a perfect clue. There is a scene when Christine describes being alone with the Phantom in his lair . . . "Presently I heard the sound of the organ; and then I began to understand Erik's contemptuous phrase when he spoke about operatic music. What I now heard was utterly different from what had charmed me up to then. His *Don Juan Triumphant* (for I had not a doubt but that he had rushed to his masterpiece to forget the horror of the moment) seemed to me at first one awful, long, magnificent sob. But, little by little, it expressed every emotion, every suffering of which mankind is capable. It intoxicated me; . . ." What a marvellous opportunity! I decided that if we adapted the plot to include a performance of an opera specially composed for Christine by the Phantom, we could not only introduce a far more modern musical ingredient in the score, but could contrive a situation where the Phantom was not only unmasked in front of many characters, but on the stage of his opera house, in his own opera, in what was supposed to be his night of triumph.'

Lloyd Webber further altered the plot. His decision to follow the romantic strain of the Leroux novel led to his structuring the denouement of the musical as a trio between Raoul, Christine and the Phantom. It was this decision that led him to remove the character of the Persian, the torture chamber and Raoul's brother. Lloyd Webber was interested primarily in the relationship between the three protagonists. The character of Mme Giry was also altered and she became the starchy mistress of the ballet, with her daughter Meg as one of the petite rats, as the dancing chorus girls were known. Charles Hart observed that there was no intention to follow the embellished, travestied storyline of movie versions, nor conversely, to make it seem like a faithful BBC classic serial.

Supporting Hal Prince for the musical staging and dance sequences was Gillian Lynne, a former dancer who has become a major choreographer and director. Andrew Lloyd Webber had asked her to join the team, aware that she was over-qualified for the job she would do, but there was no diffidence on her part at the prospect of working with Hal Prince again. Although there is little dancing in *The Phantom of the Opera*, her presence in the team was to enrich the production. She studied the dance styles of the period, and taught the

*A*ndrew Lloyd Webber.

*S*arah Brightman.

*M*ichael Crawford.

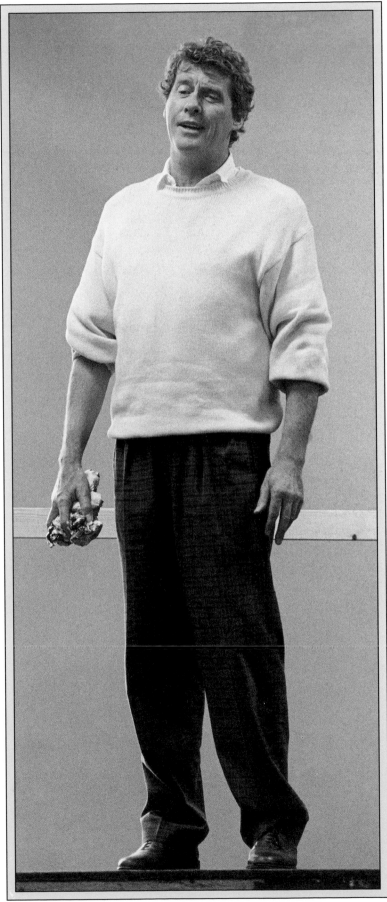

dancers in her small ballet chorus to hold themselves with their arms in front, the torso tilted forward, eschewing the exaggerated back postures and strained legs of the post-Russian ballet. Maria Björnson's cleverly designed costumes hung exactly like the tutus and ballet skirts of the 1880s, and audiences were to applaud the Degas-style poses.

There was disappointment for Steve Harley, who had hoped that the part of the Phantom would be his. Instead Lloyd Webber directed that the role should go to Michael Crawford. Lloyd Webber had heard Crawford singing when collecting Sarah Brightman from a class held by their teacher Ian Adam, and was impressed by his vocal range. Crawford, celebrated for his physically charged performance in the title role of *Barnum*, had also appeared as the juvenile lead in the film version of *Hello Dolly*, with Barbra Streisand, and in the hit show *Billy*, a musical which ran for two years at the Drury Lane theatre. In boyhood, he had sung in the English Opera Group, with Benjamin Britten casting him in the world premiere of *Noah's Flood* and *Let's Make An Opera*. In later years he became a presence in every British home with his portrayal of the well-meaning, endearing, but monumentally clumsy Frank Spencer in the television comedy series *Some Mothers Do 'Ave 'Em*. Renowned for his exacting dedication to his craft, Crawford had just gone to the West Indies, on his first holiday in four years, but after three days of frantic telephone calls from London he abandoned it to present himself to the management.

It was a brilliant casting coup. He not only had the physical agility to express himself with his body when his face was shrouded by its mask and disfiguring make-up, but as a fearless stunt performer, had no qualms about balancing precariously on a gilded angel which would soar over the audience's heads, or shooting through the dangerous stage device, the star trap. The illusionist, Paul Daniels, was brought in to devise certain magic effects which would characterize Crawford's performance. The Phantom would be able to shoot fireballs from a staff, appear and disappear at will, and at the end of the show vanish in front of the audience. Said Crawford: 'It was great to be in at the beginning of something. It has been the greatest adventure of my career without a doubt, to be there as it grew.'

Although Andrew Lloyd Webber has never made any secret of the fact that he composed the part of Christine with his wife, Sarah Brightman, in mind, her selection for the role was not a foregone conclusion, and other actresses were auditioned. It was by no means an empty exercise. The demands of the role and her physical frailty would require an understudy of comparable quality to be ready to go on at certain performances, and Claire Moore was chosen, eventually taking over as the principal Christine when, in early 1987, Sarah Brightman left the cast.

'The role of Christine is one of the most demanding I have ever written,' said her husband. 'It involves not only being able to sing music covering an enormous range for a considerable length of time, but it also demands that the artist can dance "on pointe". My Christine is a member of the corps de ballet. The Phantom believes in her voice because it represents a new sound in music, purer than a conventional soprano.'

Gillian Lynne.

Richard Stilgoe.

*M*ichael Crawford, Steve Barton and Sarah
Brightman rehearse the 'Mausoleum' scene.

*H*al Prince with Sarah Brightman and Steve Barton.

Christine's transformation from dancer to singer meant that Sarah Brightman was able to use her talents in both these areas. However, it was not easy. As Sarah Brightman explained, 'The way that I use my muscles as a dancer is quite different to the way I use them as a singer. Both methods work against each other and it was hard for me to separate the two. It is essential that Christine, a ballet girl suddenly plucked from the chorus to sing a leading role, develops her voice as the plot moves on if Andrew's idea of the character is to work. I had to control my voice and develop it as Christine would have done, so I couldn't start off too strong.'

It was the demands of the role that led to an agreement from the outset that no Christine should sing the role for more than six performances a week – a policy Lloyd Webber and Rice introduced eight years previously with *Evita* – and led to some compromises in the dancing when Brightman did not perform.

The part of Raoul was cast on the inspiration of Gillian Lynne. Several actors had been seen, but none seemed right. She had remembered a young American who had been the dance captain in one of her shows and had gone off to work in Vienna and Berlin. So she telephoned him and suggested that he arranged to get himself over to London quickly, staying at her flat so that he would only have to pay the air fare, because she had a hunch that something good was about to happen. He did as bid, and was duly auditioned. He sang 'I Am What I Am', from *La Cage aux Folles*, in German. Halfway through the test piece Hal Prince turned to Gillian Lynne and said, 'That's it!' And so Steve Barton joined the cast.

The choice of London theatre was particularly sensitive. Ideally, Lloyd Webber would have liked to have staged it in the Palace, a Victorian theatre built for Sir Arthur Sullivan as the London Opera House, and which had been bought by the Really Useful Group, but it had become home to the Cameron Mackintosh/RSC production of *Les Misérables*, which was destined for a very long run. The smaller Her Majesty's was available, however, and although in recent years it had not sustained any long-running hits it had been the venue for the original London production of *West Side Story* in 1958, and *Fiddler on the Roof*, which opened in 1967 and played for 2,030 performances. The present theatre, the fourth on the site, was completed in 1897 for the actor-manager, Herbert Tree. The building in the Haymarket is an exquisite example of late Victorian theatre architecture, and the only house left in the West End with its original wooden machinery still intact beneath the stage. Its character was, they felt, exactly suited to the mood of the show, and Maria Björnson incorporated some of its decorative features into her own decor, constructing a projecting rococo proscenium in front of the real one, although Lloyd Webber had considerable misgivings as Her Majestys theatre was the scene of his disastrous musical *Jeeves*, written with Alan Ayckbourn in 1975.

The chandelier effect was carefully worked out. During the prologue, set at an auction on the stage of the Paris Opéra many years after the main action, the audience watch as a crumpled pile of glass and brass is hoisted aloft, transforming as it ascends into a magnificent, iridescent mass and the scene changes to the same theatre in its heyday decades earlier. The climax of Act I brings this same

*H*al *Prince.*

chandelier plunging down to land on the stage in front of Christine, an effect achieved by a cat's cradle of invisible wires and two electric motors. The local authority inspectors carefully scrutinized the operation of this effect to ensure that a real disaster cannot happen.

Maria Björnson built the sets in miniature and displayed them in a model of the stage area. Prince prefers to use a model for his blocking, and knows in advance of rehearsals what he wants. His technique is greatly admired, especially by Andrew Lloyd Webber.

'The first thing that Hal does is to sit the cast down in front of the model and say this is the set and this is how it should be done. I've never seen any other director work like that. He is extraordinarily visual. I remember him saying once that a score isn't right unless it looks right.

Hal Prince gently imposed his vision on the show. 'The music should be pounding on, taking you to the next place, a kind of pulse that keeps pulling at you. That appealed to Andrew, and the show often does that.

'I was watching a BBC programme called *The Skin Horse* about people who were physically incapacitated, or deformed, a series of interviews with quadraplegics, Thalidomide victims, talking about what it was like, and I sensed that the thing that united them all was a very normal, healthy sexuality. And that's what Maria and I wanted to put up there, and it affected the design of the proscenium, with its statues intertwined in some moment of passion which the audiences sees and absorbs.

'It's not a simple show, but it's not an enormous technological show. We took advantage of the working Victorian machinery – we could have staged it in the same way had we opened when the theatre was first built. In New York we shall adapt the Majestic Theatre in a similar way. We wanted to do something that would *only* work in the theatre.' Andrew Bridge's superb lighting exactly matched that aim.

Few shows have generated so much anticipation. Ticket sales were already booming as soon as they became available, and long before the opening many performances were sold out. Advance bookings are a satisfying cushion if the critical notices turn out badly, and often expensively mounted successes have survived an initial lack of enthusiasm. Nevertheless, no producer is happy if the press is hostile.

The Phantom of the Opera in its latter stages of pre-production proved to be remarkably newsworthy. Speculation raged over every facet of casting and every minor hitch in the staging. Exaggerated stories were rife, and non-existent disasters were assiduously reported. Something called the curse of the Phantom was invoked to explain away the predictable setbacks that hinder the staging of any major production and which are usually ironed out by the official first night.

For *The Phantom of the Opera* it was Thursday, 9 October 1986, following a short period of previews, not all of which, as the press scrupulously noted, had run smoothly. The critics were impressed. Any doubts regarding the suitability of Michael Crawford and Sarah Brightman in the key roles were allayed. As a duo they worked perfectly together. Crawford's discipline and energy made him seem ubiquitous, a presence pervading the atmosphere even when not on stage. His tender and hypnotic singing voice, and the

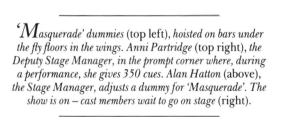

'*Masquerade*' *dummies* (top left), *hoisted on bars under the fly floors in the wings.* Anni Partridge (top right), *the Deputy Stage Manager, in the prompt corner where, during a performance, she gives 350 cues.* Alan Hatton (above), *the Stage Manager, adjusts a dummy for '*Masquerade*'. The show is on – cast members wait to go on stage* (right).

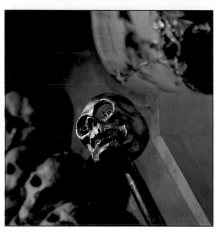

The wigroom at Her Majesty's Theatre (top left). Wigs (top right), prepared and ready for a performance. The skull head staff (above), from which the Phantom shoots fireballs. Left: the musical box – a figure of a monkey in Persian robes playing the cymbals – whose quaint, haunting theme recurs throughout the production reminding us of the tender relationship between Christine and the Phantom.

A dressing-room scene at Her Majesty's (opposite). Organized chaos gives way to another perfect performance. Right: the ballet girls are instructed by Madame Giry. Their tutus are made of 12 metres of tarlatan, a kind of stiffened muslin, as were the original tutus of the Dégas period. The layers of skirt are edged using pinking scissors. The bodice is made of linen. Each girl used 12 pairs of ballet shoes per month.

Michael Crawford being lowered in the Angel for the 'Roof of the Opera House' scene.

tortured body movements of a man constrained emotionally and physically, gripped the audience with as powerful a hold as that of Erik over Christine. Sarah Brightman fulfilled all expectations in a role skilfully fashioned for her by her husband, and delighted the audience with the precision and clarity of her bell-like soprano.

Of the whole Company, Lloyd Webber said, 'It was one of the strongest I had ever worked with. It was very exciting as it was really the first time I had been involved with so many artists who came almost exclusively from an operatic background.' The Lloyd Webber score proved to be strongly atmospheric, lushly romantic and also knowingly witty. Meeting head-on those who had scorned his talent for pastiche, he delighted in faking part of a Meyerbeer-esque grand opera, *Hannibal*, with a scenic elephant, a demented soprano and a chorus of slave girls, and in the Sitzprobe for the Phantom's opera, which is written in the whole tone scale, he revels in Signor Piangi being unable to master the tonality accurately. The audience went home to spend days with their heads filled with some of the insidious melodies such as 'Music of the Night', 'All I Ask of You' and 'Past the Point of No Return', whilst the final trio and the sextet for Carlotta, Piangi, Raoul, Mme Giry and the Opera Managers are perhaps the most accomplished pieces of musical construction he has composed to date.

Among the many technical complications was the make-up of the Phantom. Christopher Tucker, who had devised the deformed features displayed by John Hurt in the film *The Elephant Man*, was engaged to design a horrific head which had to be applied to Crawford's own features six times a week. There were endless journeys from London to Tucker's Berkshire base for a period of three months. The design could not have the subtlety of film make-up, but instead had to be capable of making the audience even at the back of the upper circle recoil in disgust, without forfeiting sympathy for the misshapen Erik. At the same time the make-up could not be so overpowering as to prevent him from acting. An inspired addition was a vertical half-mask which left part of Crawford's face always visible. A Lon Chaney approach, with cheek padding on the inside, would have made singing impossible. 'We tried it, but I sounded like Marlon Brando in *The Godfather*,' said Crawford, 'and I can't have anything in my ears because I must hear the music.' Contact lenses, however, diminish his vision to such an extent that in some scenes he has to be led on to the stage.

The physical discomfort of the double layers of latex and the wig, particularly on days when there are two performances, proved to be acute. 'It's like being trapped in a lift – it's quite horrendous,' said Crawford. After the show had been running for a few months, he had managed to get the application stage reduced from nearly three hours to just under two.

Daily preparation for the role of the Phantom goes far beyond the application of layers of grotesque make-up. Every aspect of the costuming was carefully worked out with Maria Björnson, including footwear, consisting of tight-fitting boots extending above the ankles, giving his feet a pinched, narrow appearance, and a strained, delicate gait. The Phantom's shirt is designed to button between the legs so that when he stretches against the portcullis in his lair it does not ride

*T*he dummies for 'Masquerade' (above left) are set in position on the Grand Staircase. A stagehand supervises the Grand Staircase (above), folding away to lie flat against the back wall of the stage at the end of 'Masquerade'. The false stage (left), the 'audience' applaud Christine as she takes her bow after her Gala opening night. View of the orchestra (below left), with musical director, Michael Reed.

up and destroy the smooth symmetry of his shape.

As Michael Crawford testifies, 'I feel incredibly sorry for Erik, I feel terrific compassion for him. And I think that the audience must also, because I have never seen such a reaction from men and women alike. They enjoy it in an emotional way. It's as though anyone who has ever felt love will come out crying. They feel sympathy towards that man's plea, that cry he makes at the end. Even Kate, my dresser, wept when she saw it. I felt it all from the music Andrew wrote – from day one, when he played the first six bars, that was when I felt the man for the first time. It was the overture, and every night when it starts up it still puts the hair on the back of my hand on end. As I hear it coming over the sound system I stand up in the dressing room for it, it's just like the anthem to me.'

In common with most people in the theatre Crawford has a number of personal superstitions, and likes to maintain a consistent routine as the time of his first entrance approaches. 'I have a ritual every night, and it's always the same. I sit on the edge of the table and then I stand up as that music starts and I look into the mirror, and I see the man. That's his music, and I'm ready then. Ready to go down and start.' Another important aspect was the physical look of Christine. The role as perceived by Lloyd Webber demanded that Christine be a convincing member of the corps de ballet; a physique which is not normally associated with operatic sopranos! As Sarah Brightman explained, 'In order to prepare for the performance, I found I needed at least three hours prior to curtain up to allow me time for a complete physical, vocal and mental warm-up.'

Each night a large and talented team of backstage staff work in unison to ensure a smooth performance. The wings of Her Majesty's are cramped, and parts of sets are carefully stowed in every available spare inch of space until the moment when they are needed. Everything must have its place. There are travelators, or moving platforms, which turn into ramps to allow Christine and the Phantom

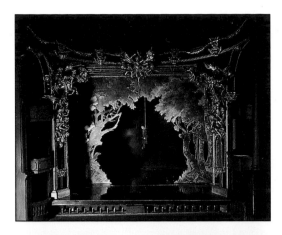

to descend to his lair after she has been enticed through the dressing-room mirror. Not one but two sets of doubles sharpen the impact of this key scene.

The great curving staircase for the masked ball number, 'Masquerade', is folded, concertina-style, to stand flush against the rear stage wall, and overhead the costumed dummies that augment the live revellers hang like rows of bizarre corpses dangling from a gibbet. All through the single interval, while the cast rest and the audience rush for refreshment, a precision team of stagehands, each drilled in a specific task, construct from scratch Maria Björnson's impressionistic version of the Opéra foyer. The staircase unfolds and then the set is silently peopled, first by the dummies on poles thrust through holes in the set, later by the cast, and invariably, as the curtain rises for the second act, the audience applaud the eerie beauty of the scene. The Phantom appears in his striking crimson costume as Red Death, and another double enables an astonishing vanishing trick to be enacted. Crawford has to be hoisted to the top of the 'Masquerade' staircase by means of a forklift, and it is his least favourite entrance in the show since the costume and mask render him almost blind.

At the end of the show the release from tension for everyone is palpable. A good night is one that has played hitch-free in spite of the thousands of things that can go wrong. Should any of the mechanical devices fail, such as the boat or the travelators, there are agreed procedures to span the gap without the audience sensing that anything is wrong, but rarely have they been invoked.

Part of the success of *The Phantom of the Opera*, launched in London and destined for the world, is a consequence of the creative fusion of some of the most notable talents currently at work in the theatre. A group that, with the conquest of London safely achieved, moved on to secure New York, where the Majestic Theatre on West 44th Street was structurally transformed, with a new proscenium and an even more threatening chandelier than at Her Majesty's. The London production cost £2 million, of which £900,000 was the budget for the Björnson sets and costumes, but given the escalating price of major musical productions it is by no means an outrageous figure. New York in the winter of 1988 was securely gripped by phantomania and the first night on 26 January was the stuff of Broadway legend.

There is another factor in the success of *The Phantom of the Opera*, that of timing. Lloyd Webber's gifts include a true theatrical instinct, not only in knowing how to hold an audience in performance, but also in his ability to sense that the day of the spiky, abrasive, loose-structured musical may well have passed, and that there is a public thirsting for extravagant romance, colourful spectacle, proscenium arches, orchestra pits, helpless heroines, rugged heroes, tragic villains and evocative melodies. It is that insight into prevailing tastes, which is then met with offerings of impeccable quality, that he has in common with Steven Spielberg, the most successful director in the history of the cinema.

The Lloyd Webber *Phantom* in the cinema? He is reticent. 'I am a theatrical animal,' said Lloyd Webber in a recent interview with David Frost. But, Lloyd Webber in the cinema with a fine director! It could just give us the definitive version of the Leroux legend.

A selection of Maria Björnson's costume designs. (Clockwise from top left) male singers in the 'Hannibal' scene: the female chorus for 'Hannibal'; the Managers; slavemasters in the 'Hannibal' scene.

A selection of Maria Björnson's 'Masquerade' designs.

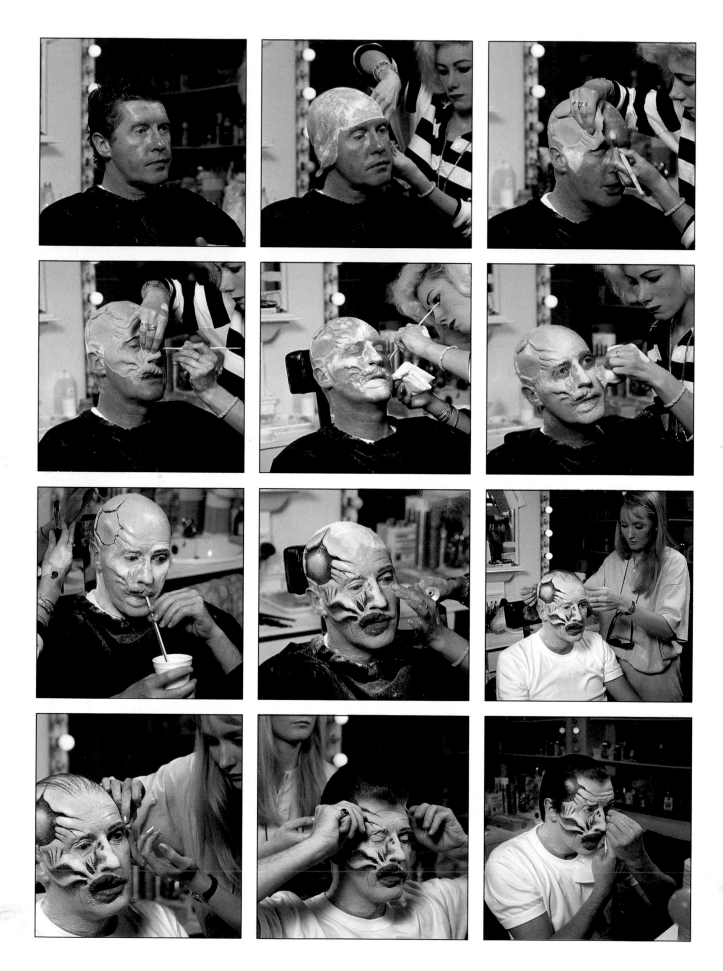

Michael Crawford has his make-up applied by Tiffany Hicks. The daily procedure takes approximately two hours, but before it begins, the face must be moisturized and the hair wetted down, the face shaved very closely and, every two or three days, the neck as well. Once the glue is applied to the prosthetics (the foam latex pieces that make up the Phantom's face), they cannot be altered as they set in place immediately. After one hour, Tiffany paints, highlights and shades the Phantom's face, and two wigs are fitted, together with the radio mike. Last of all, the two contact lenses (one white and one dark blue) are put in. After the performance, the make-up is removed very carefully with oil and a brush. Great care must be taken not to damage the skin because, if injured, it has no chance to heal before the next performance.

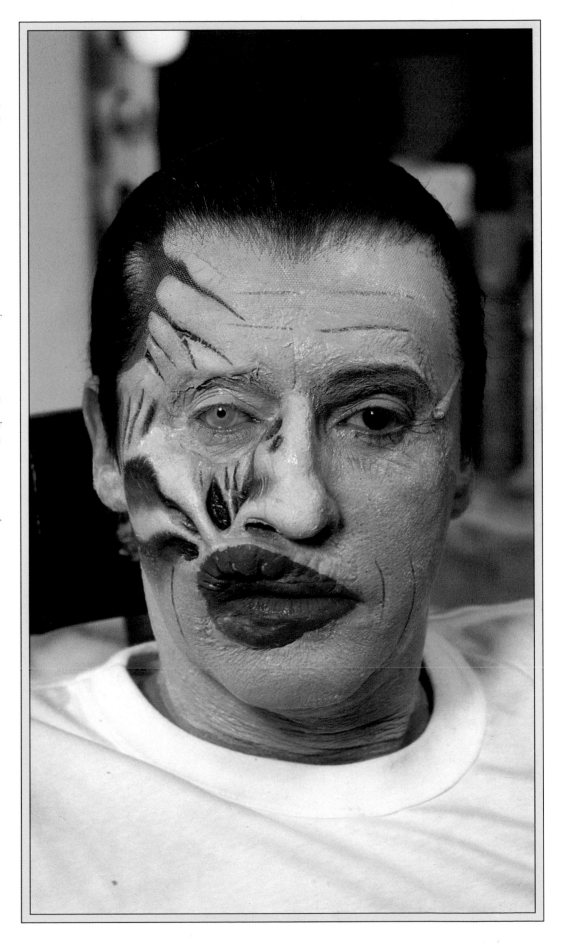

The principals, photographed by Terry O'Neill before opening night.

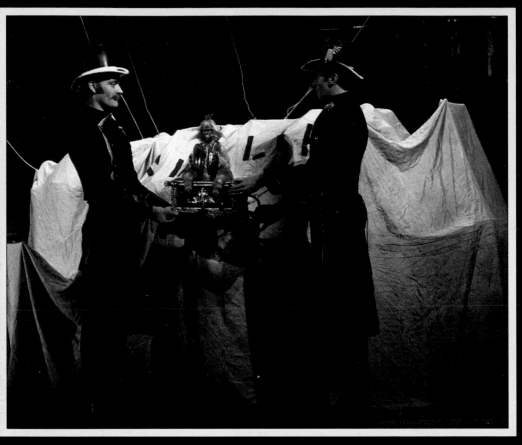

The stage set for the start of Act 1– 'the Auction' (left). The chandelier is hoisted upwards as the drapes fly, and the Phantom's theme is heard for the first time (below left). One of the drapes from Act I (opposite). This was specially dyed and printed from an original design. For the show, 2,230 metres of fabric were used for the drapes, 900 of them specially dyed. The tasselled fringes amount to 226 metres made up of 250 kilos of dyed wool with 5,000 wooden balls, imported from India, interwoven. Each one is handmade and combed through with an Afro comb.

The chandelier in the production weighs three-quarters of a ton and was built by five people in four weeks. It is made up of 6,000 beads, 35 beads to each string. Separating each bead are three knots; if a knot becomes loose there is the back-up from the other two knots to prevent the beads from falling into the auditorium. It is regularly inspected by the local authorities for safety purposes.

'*Hannibal*' (left). *A shot of the 'Hannibal' elephant* (right), *taken from the flys. John Aron* (below right) *as Piangi playing 'Hannibal'.*

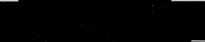

Raoul and the Managers watch Christine (top). Christine sings at her Gala 'Think of Me . . .' (middle). Christine and Raoul meet in her dressing-room after her Gala (bottom).

Meg asks Christine about the teacher who has taught her to sing so beautifully (opposite).

*The Phantom takes
Christine 'through' the
mirror of her dressing-
room. The mirror
dissolves as she
disappears into it,
leaving her room
empty . . .*

" Every wave is a watersprite who swims in the current, each current is a path which snakes towards my palace, and my palace is fluidly built at the bottom of the lake, in the triangle of earth, fire and water. "

EMILE ZOLA

The journey to the Phantom's lair (left). Michael Crawford as the Phantom (right).

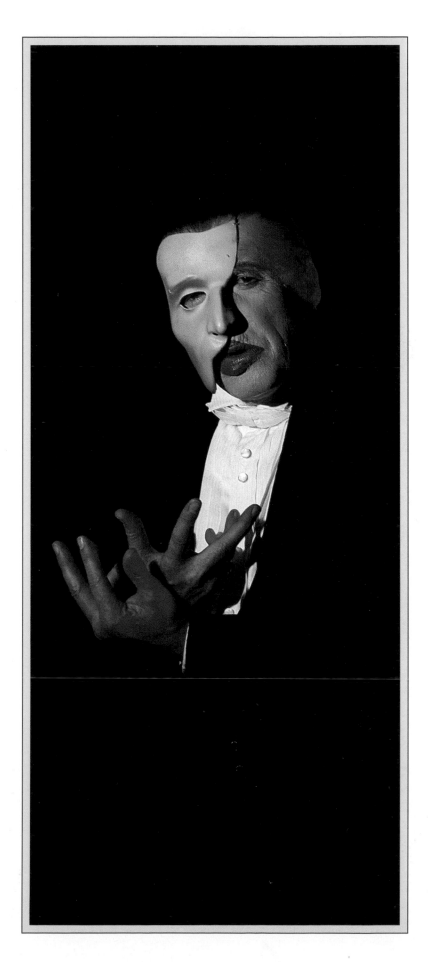

The Phantom induces Christine to sing to his will. Inset: Christine, terrified, gives the Phantom back his mask.

The Phantom bewitches Christine (opposite) *with his power over her voice. Buquet, Chief of the Flys* (right), *tells the ballet girls tales of the Opéra Ghost. Later, the Phantom takes his revenge and Buquet will hang from the flys. 'Dance of the Country Nymphs'* (below right). *Flickers of light from the Phantom's lantern are visible through the backcloth.*

'Il Muto' – *the cuckolded old man (top). The costumes for 'Il Muto' and 'Don Juan' are made up, using new fabrics as a base, with old material sewn over it to give an antique look. The old man's coat is made of antique satin panels from India embroidered with silver. Rosemary Ashe plays Carlotta (above). A quick change for the 'Il Muto' scene necessitates swift action from dressers waiting behind the bedhead, out of sight of the audience. The Managers and Carlotta reproach the Opéra Ghost (right).*

*T*he angel sculpture.
The Phantom delivers his
commands from the angel
(opposite).

*"Glory remains
unaware of my
neglected dwelling
where alone I sing my
tearful song
which has
charms only for me."*

CHARLES BRUGNOT

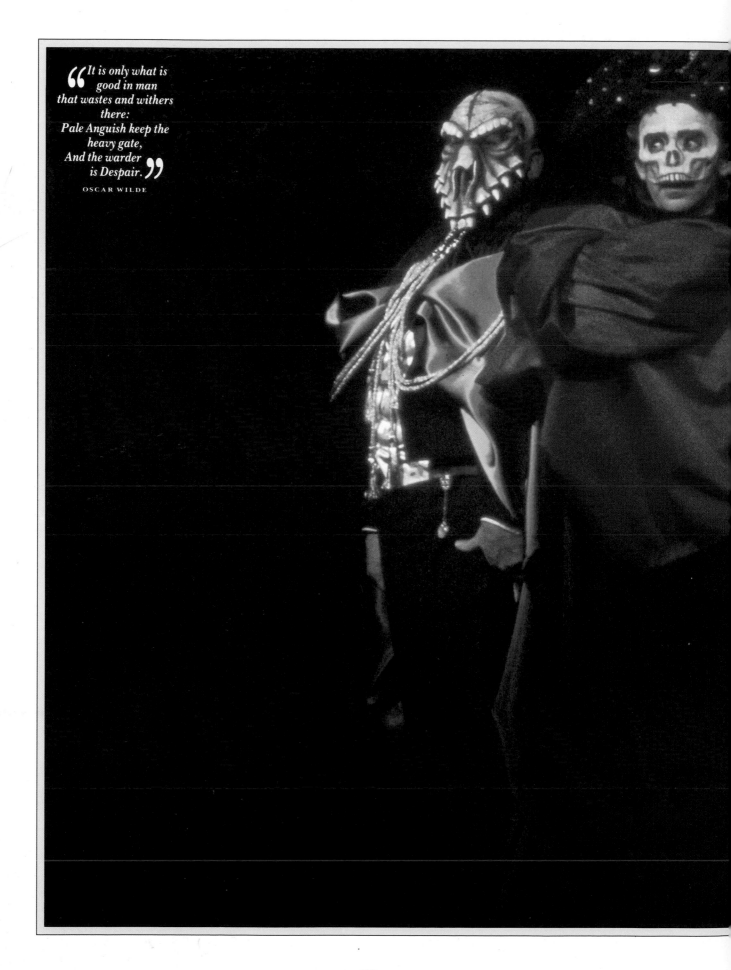

"It is only what is good in man that wastes and withers there: Pale Anguish keep the heavy gate, And the warder is Despair."

OSCAR WILDE

The Managers (left), hide behind their 'Masquerade' costumes. Above: Scenes from 'Masquerade'.

'Masquerade'

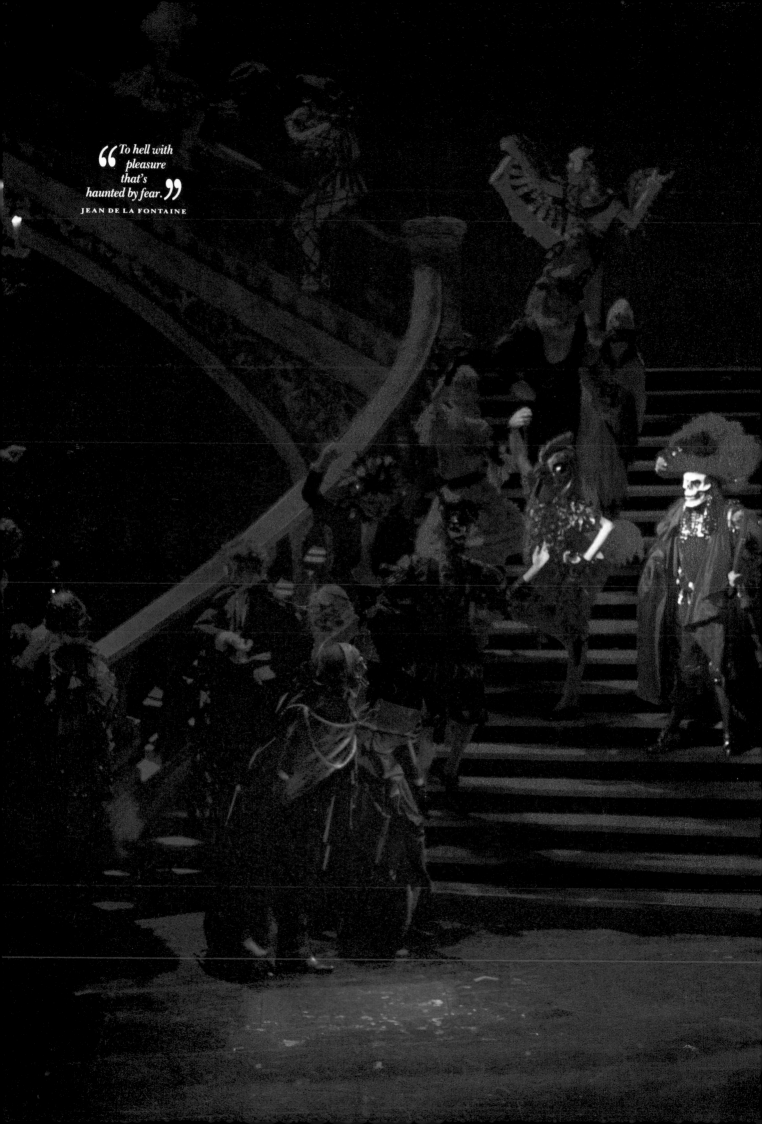

> *To hell with pleasure that's haunted by fear.*
>
> **JEAN DE LA FONTAINE**

The Phantom walks down the Grand Staircase in the Red Death mask, scattering the guests. Christine stands paralysed by his approach. Inset: The Phantom and Christine meet. He pulls off the secret engagement chain given to her by Raoul – 'Your chains are still mine . . .'

The 'Monkey Girl'
costume (right) from
'Masquerade'. A detail
from some of the fine
materials used (below).
The dual sex costume
(far right) was made by a
husband and wife team.
The male half was made
up by the husband, an
experienced tailor, while
his wife, a dress-maker,
attached the female part.

A selection of 'Masquerade' costumes. All the costumes were designed by Maria Björnson, and supervised by Sue Wilmington. They were made up by 35 different costumiers from all over Britain.

There are approximately 12–15 metres of fabric and 60 metres of braid in each costume. They are minutely detailed and meticulously put together.

More costumes by Maria Björnson. With a few exceptions, most of the cast have approximately seven costume changes. The 'Masquerade' costumes incorporate fabrics and accessories bought in Southall, West London, where there is a large Indian community. So much braid was purchased over the weeks of preparation that the costume supervisor's car became known as the 'braidmobile'!

Complementing the costumes, there are a total of 150 wigs used in the show — five people have to work daily on them starting at 10.00 in the morning. For instance, Christine's wig is made of real hair and has to be rolled up on sticks to be set. This takes one hour. It is then baked in the 'oven' for five hours, after which it is combed out and styled to give the sensational pre-Raphaelite look.

Don't be fooled into thinking there is a real person in this costume. It is, in fact, a dummy!

Christine (opposite) sings 'Wishing you were somehow here again . . .'

The Phantom has composed a new opera. Christine (top), rails 'I cannot sing it/Duty or not . . .' Piangi at the rehearsal for the Phantom's opera experiences difficulty with his notes (above).

"That lovely voice; how I should weep for joy if I could hear it now!"
COLETTE

The Phantom in the Mausoleum, shoots fireballs from the head of his staff to frighten Raoul and Christine.

> **"** *I do not despair in the least of ultimate triumph. I repeat it with intense conviction.* **"**
>
> EMILE ZOLA

Christine and Raoul on the roof of the Opéra. Right: 'Bravo Monsieur . . .' the Phantom ridicules Raoul.

Christine in the opening scene from 'Don Juan' (right). Piangi is discovered dead behind the curtain of the alcove in 'Don Juan' (below right).

The Phantom and Christine (opposite). He sings 'Past the Point of No Return . . .' Christine listens, horrified at the intensity of his words.

Christine kisses the Phantom. Inset: Raoul and Christine embrace each other either side of the Phantom's portcullis.

*The Phantom watches
in despair from behind
his portcullis as Christine
and Raoul disappear
across the lake.*

> *The best laid plot can injure its maker, and often a man's perfidy will rebound on himself.*
>
> **JEAN DE LA FONTAINE**

*The fire which
seems out
often sleeps
beneath the cinders.*
PIERRE CORNEILLE

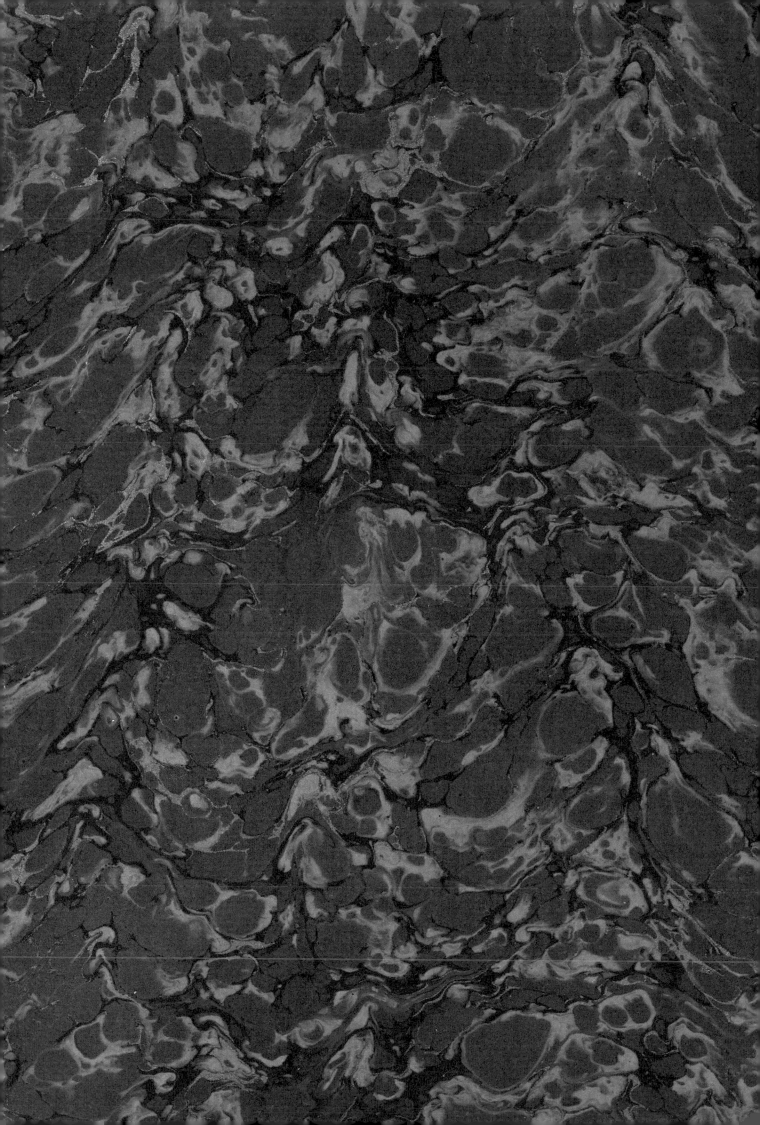

THE
LIBRETTO

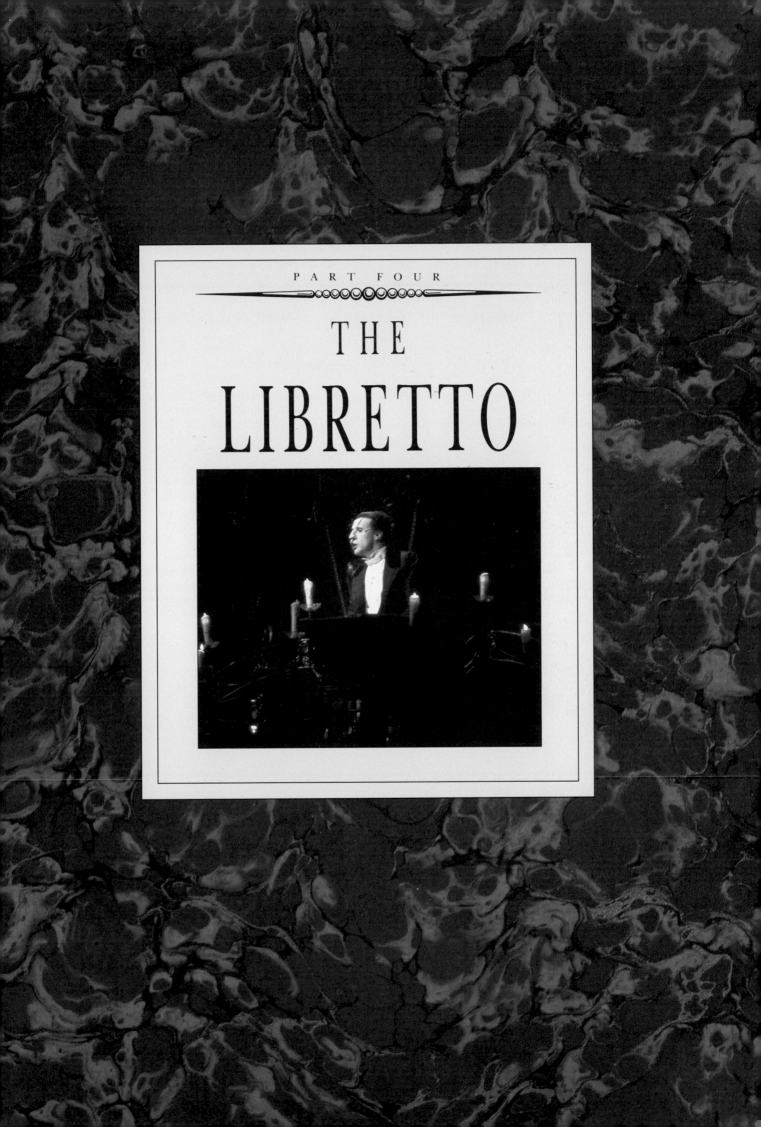

C O N T E N T S

PROLOGUE
The stage of the Paris Opéra, 1905

Auctioneer, Raoul and Company
OVERTURE

ENTR'ACTE

ACT ONE – PARIS 1881

ACT TWO – Six months later

PROLOGUE

THE STAGE OF THE PARIS OPÉRA, 1905
(The contents of the opera house is being auctioned off.
An AUCTIONEER, PORTERS, BIDDERS and RAOUL, seventy now, but still bright of eye.
The action commences with a blow from the AUCTIONEER's gavel)

AUCTIONEER
Sold. Your number sir? Thank you.

Lot 663, then, ladies and gentlemen: a poster for this house's production of 'Hannibal' by Chalumeau.

PORTER
Showing here.

AUCTIONEER
Do I have ten francs? Five then, Five I am bid. Six, seven. Against you, sir, seven. Eight. Eight once. Selling twice. Sold, to Raoul, Vicomte de Chagny.

Lot 664: a wooden pistol and three human skulls, from the 1831 production of 'Robert le Diable" by Meyerbeer. Ten francs for this. Ten, thank you. Ten francs still. Fifteen, thank you, sir. Fifteen I am bid. Going at fifteen.
Your number, Sir?

Lot 665, ladies and gentlemen: a papier-mâché musical box, in the shape of a barrel-organ. Attached, the figure of a monkey in Persian robes, playing the cymbals. This item, discovered in the vaults of the theatre, still in working order.

PORTER *(holding it up)*
Showing here. *(He sets it in motion)*

AUCTIONEER
May I start at twenty francs? Fifteen, then? Fifteen I am bid.

(The bidding continues. RAOUL eventually buys the box for thirty francs)

Sold, for thirty francs to the Vicomte de Chagny. Thank you sir.

(The box is handed across to RAOUL. He studies it, as attention focuses on him for a moment)

RAOUL *(quietly, half to himself, half to the box)*
A collector's
piece indeed ...
every detail
exactly as she said ...

She often
spoke of you, my friend ...
your velvet lining
and your figurine of lead ...

Will you still play, when
all the rest of us are dead ...?

(Attention returns to the AUCTIONEER, as he resumes)

AUCTIONEER
Lot 666, then: a chandelier in pieces. Some of you may recall the strange affair of the Phantom of the Opera: a mystery never fully explained. We are told, ladies and gentlemen, that this is the very chandelier which figures in the famous disaster. Our workshops have restored it and fitted up parts of it with wiring for the new electric light, so that we may get a hint of what it may look like when re-assembled. Perhaps we may frighten away the ghost of so many years ago with a little illumination, gentlemen?

(The AUCTIONEER switches on the chandelier. There is an enormous flash, and the OVERTURE begins. During the overture the opera house is restored to its earlier grandeur. The chandelier, immense and glittering, rises magically from the stage, finally hovering high above the stalls)

ALL BOLD TYPE INDICATES SUNG LINES.

VARIATIONS IN THE LIBRETTO
OCCUR DURING A PERFORMANCE.

ACT ONE

Scene 1

REHEARSALS FOR 'HANNIBAL' BY CHALUMEAU

(We have reached the great choral scene in which HANNIBAL and his army return to save Carthage from the Roman invasion under Scipio. HANNIBAL is UBALDO PIANGI; ELISSA, Queen of Carthage (his mistress) is CARLOTTA GIUDICELLI. The two leading SLAVE GIRLS are played by MEG GIRY and CHRISTINE DAAÉ. MME GIRY is the ballet mistress. M. REYER, the répétiteur, is in charge,

We join the opera towards the end of ELISSA's (CARLOTTA's) great aria. She is alone, holding a present from the approaching HANNIBAL, a bleeding severed head)

CARLOTTA *(at the climax of an extravagant cadenza)*

This trophy from our saviours,
from the enslaving force
of Rome!

(A STAGE HAND carries a ladder across the stage. OTHERS are seen still constructing parts of the scenery)

GIRLS' CHORUS
With feasting and dancing and song,
tonight in celebration,
we greet the victorious throng,
returned to bring salvation!

MEN'S CHORUS
The trumpets of Carthage resound!
Hear, Romans, now and tremble!
Hark to our step on the ground!

ALL
Hear the drums –
Hannibal comes!

(PIANGI enters, as HANNIBAL)

PIANGI *(HANNIBAL)*
Sad to return to find the land we love
threatened once more by Roma's far-reaching
grasp.

REYER *(interrupting him)*
Signor ... If you please; 'Rome'. We say
'Rome', not 'Roma'.

PIANGI
Si, si, Rome, not Roma. Is very hard for me.
(practising) Rome ... Rome ...

(Enter LEFÈVRE, the retiring manager of the Opéra, with M. FIRMIN and M. ANDRÉ to whom he has just sold it)

REYER *(to PIANGI)*
Once again, then if you please, Signor: 'Sad to
return ...'

LEFÈVRE *(to ANDRÉ and FIRMIN)*
This way, gentlemen, this way. Rehearsals, as
you see, are under way, for a new production
of Chalumeau's 'Hannibal'.

(Sensing a hiatus in the rehearsal, LEFÈVRE attempts to attract attention)

LEFÈVRE
Ladies and gentlemen, some of you may
already, perhaps, have met M. André and M.
Firmin ...

(The new managers are politely bowing, when REYER interrupts)

REYER
I'm sorry, M. Lefèvre, we *are* rehearsing. If
you wouldn't mind waiting a moment?

LEFÈVRE
My apologies. M. Reyer, Proceed, proceed ...

REYER
Thank you, monsieur. *(turning back to PIANGI).*
'Sad to return ...', Signor ...

LEFÈVRE *(sotto voce to ANDRÉ and FIRMIN)*
M. Reyer, our chief répétiteur. Rather a
tyrant, I'm afraid.

(The rehearsal continues)

PIANGI *(HANNIBAL)*
Sad to return to find the land we love
threatened once more by Rome's far-reaching
grasp.
Tomorrow we shall break the chains of Rome.
Tonight, rejoice – your army has come home.

(The BALLET GIRLS begin their dance. LEFÈVRE, ANDRÉ and FIRMIN stand centre-stage watching the ballet. They are in the way. The ballet continues under the following dialogue)

LEFÈVRE *(indicating PIANGI)*
Signor Piangi, our principal tenor. He does
play so well opposite La Carlotta.

GIRY *(exasperated by their presence, bangs her cane angrily on the stage)*
Gentlemen, please! If you would kindly move
to one side?

LEFÈVRE
My apologies, Mme. Giry.
(leading ANDRÉ and FIRMIN aside)
Madame Giry, our ballet mistress. I don't
mind confessing, M. Firmin, I shan't be sorry
to be rid of the whole blessed business.

FIRMIN
I keep asking you, monsieur, why exactly are
you retiring?

LEFÈVRE *(ignoring this, calls his attention to the continuing ballet)*
We take a particular pride here in the
excellence of our ballets.

(MEG becomes prominent among the dancers)

ANDRÉ
Who's that girl, Lefèvre?

LEFÈVRE
Her? Meg Giry, Madame Giry's daughter.
Promising dancer. M. André, most promising.

(CHRISTINE becomes prominent. She has absent-mindedly fallen out-of-step)

GIRY *(spotting her, bangs her cane again)*
You! Christine Daaé! Concentrate, girl!

MEG *(quietly, to CHRISTINE)*
Christine ... What's the matter?

FIRMIN *(to LEFÈVRE)*
Daaé? Curious name.

LEFÈVRE
Swedish.

ANDRÉ
Any relation to the violinist?

LEFÈVRE
His daughter, I believe. Always has her head
in the clouds, I'm afraid.

(The ballet continues to its climax and ends. The CHORUS resumes)

CHORUS
Bid welcome to Hannibal's guests –
the elephants of Carthage!
As guides on our conquering quests,
Dido sends
Hannibal's friends!

(The ELEPHANT, a life-size mechanical replica, enters. PIANGI is lifted, in triumph, onto its back)

CARLOTTA *(ELISSA)*
Once more to my
welcoming arms
my love returns
in splendour!

PIANGI *(HANNIBAL)*
Once more to those
sweetest of charms
my heart and soul
surrender!

CHORUS

The trumpeting elephants sound –
hear, Romans, now and tremble!
Hark to their step on the ground –
hear the drums!
Hannibal comes!

(At the end of the chorus LEFÈVRE claps his hands for silence. The elephant is led off. Two stage-hands are revealed operating it from within)

LEFÈVRE
Ladies and gentlemen – Madame Giry, thank
you – may I have your attention please?
As you know, for some weeks there have been
rumours of my imminent retirement.
I can now tell you that these were all true, and
it is my pleasure to introduce to you the two
gentlemen who now own the Opéra
Populaire, M. Richard Firmin and M. Gilles
André.

(Polite applause. Some bowing. CARLOTTA makes her presence felt)

Gentlemen, Signora Carlotta Guidicelli, our
leading soprano for five seasons now.

ANDRÉ
Of course, of course. I have experienced all
your greatest rôles, Signora.

LEFÈVRE
And Signor Ubaldo Piangi.

FIRMIN
An honour, Signor.

ANDRÉ
If I remember rightly, Elissa has a rather fine
aria in Act Three of 'Hannibal'. I wonder,
Signora, if, as a personal favour, you would
oblige us with a private rendition? *(Somewhat acerbic).* Unless, of course, M. Reyer objects
...

CARLOTTA
My manager commands . . . M. Reyer?

REYER
My diva commands. Will two bars be sufficient introduction?

FIRMIN
Two bars will be quite sufficient.

REYER *(ensuring that CARLOTTA is ready)*
Signora?

CARLOTTA
Maestro.

(The introduction is played on the piano)

CARLOTTA

Think of me,
think of me fondly,
when we've said
goodbye.
Remember me
once in a while –
please promise me
you'll try.

When you find
that, once
again, you long
to take your heart . . .

(As CARLOTTA is singing, a backdrop crashes to the floor, cutting her off from half the cast)

MEG/BALLET GIRLS/CHORUS

He's here:
the Phantom of the Opera . . .
He is with us . . .
It's the ghost . . .

PIANGI *(looking up, furiously)*
You idiots!
(He rushes over to CARLOTTA)
Cara! Cara! Are you hurt?

LEFÈVRE
Signora! Are you all right? Buquet! Where is Buquet?

PIANGI
Is no one concerned for our prima donna?

LEFÈVRE
Get that man down here! *(to ANDRÉ and FIRMIN)*
Chief of the flies. He's responsible for this.

(The drop is raised high enough to reveal upstage an old stagehand, JOSEPH BUQUET, holding a length of rope, which looks almost like a noose)

LEFÈVRE
Buquet! For God's sake, man, what's going on up there?

BUQUET
Please, monsieur,
don't look at me:
as God's my witness,
I was not at my post.

Please, monsieur,
there's no one there:
and if there is, well
then, it *must* be a ghost . . .

MEG *(looking up)*
He's there: the Phantom of the Opera . . .

ANDRÉ

Good heavens!
Will you show a little courtesy?

FIRMIN *(to MEG and the OTHERS)*
Mademoiselle, please!

ANDRÉ *(to CARLOTTA.*
These things do happen.

CARLOTTA
Si! These things *do* happen! Well, until you stop these things happening, *this* thing does *not* happen!
Ubaldo! Andiamo!
(PIANGI dutifully fetches her furs from the wings)

PIANGI
Amateurs!

LEFÈVRE
I don't think there's much more to assist you, gentlemen. Good luck. If you need me, I shall be in Frankfurt.
(He leaves. The COMPANY looks anxiously at the NEW MANAGERS)

ANDRÉ
La Carlotta will be back.

GIRY
You think so, messieurs? I have a message, sir, from the Opera Ghost.
(The GIRLS twitter and twirl in fear)

FIRMIN
God in Heaven, you're all obsessed!

GIRY
He merely welcomes you to his opera house and commands you to continue to leave Box Five empty for his use and reminds you that his salary is due.

FIRMIN
His salary?

GIRY
Monsieur Lefèvre paid him twenty thousand francs a month. Perhaps you can afford more, with the Vicomte de Chagny as your patron.
(Reaction to this from the BALLET GIRLS. CHRISTINE takes hold of MEG nervously)

ANDRÉ *(to GIRY)*
Madame, I had hoped to have made that announcement myself.

GIRY *(to FIRMIN)*
Will the Vicomte be at the performance tonight, monsieur?

FIRMIN
In our box.

ANDRÉ
Madame, who is the understudy for this rôle?

REYER
There is no understudy, monsieur – the production is new.

MEG

Christine Daaé could sing it, sir.

FIRMIN

The chorus girl?

MEG *(to FIRMIN)*
She's been taking lessons from a great teacher.

ANDRÉ
From whom?

CHRISTINE *(uneasily)*
I don't know, sir . . .

FIRMIN
Oh, not you as well!
(turning to ANDRÉ)
Can you believe it? A full house – and we have to cancel!

GIRY

Let her sing for you, monsieur. She has been well taught.

REYER *(after a pause)*
From the beginning of the aria then, mamselle.

CHRISTINE

Think of me,
think of me fondly,
when we've said
goodbye.
Remember me
once in a while –
please promise me
you'll try.

FIRMIN
André, this is doing nothing for my nerves.

ANDRÉ
Don't fret, Firmin.

CHRISTINE

When you find
that, once
again, you long
to take your heart back
and be free –
if you
ever find
a moment
spare a thought
for me . . .

(Transformation to the Gala. CHRISTINE is revealed in full costume)

We never said
our love
was evergreen,
or as unchanging
as the sea –
but if
you can still
remember,
stop and think
of me . . .

Think of all the things
we've shared and seen –
don't think about the things
which might have been . . .

Think of me,
think of me waking,
silent and
resigned.

Imagine me,
trying too hard
to put you
from my mind.

Recall those days,
look back
on all those times,
think of the things
we'll never do –
there will
never be
a day, when
I won't think
of you . . .

(Applause, bravos. Prominent among the bravos, those of the young RAOUL in the MANAGERS' box)

RAOUL

Can it be?
Can it be Christine?

Bravo!

(He raises his opera-glasses)

**What a change!
You're really
not a bit
the gawkish girl
that once you were ...**

(lowering his opera-glasses)

**She may
not remember
me, but
I remember
her ...**

CHRISTINE

**We never said
our love
was evergreen,
or as unchanging
as the sea –
but please
promise me,
that sometimes,
you will think
of me!**

Scene 2
AFTER THE GALA

(The curtain closes upstage. BALLET GIRLS, from the wings, gush around CHRISTINE who hands each a flower from her bouquet. REYER stiffly gives his approval)

GIRY *(to CHRISTINE)*
Yes, you did well. He will be pleased.
(To the DANCERS)
And you! You were a disgrace tonight!
Such *ronds de jambe!*
Such *temps de cuisse!*
Here – we rehearse. Now!
*(She emphasizes this with her cane.
The BALLET GIRLS settle into rehearsal upstage,
GIRY keeping time with her stick. Variations of this
continue throughout the scene)*

*(CHRISTINE moves slowly, downstage, away from the
DANCERS, as her dressing room becomes visible. Unseen
by her, MEG also moves away and follows her. As
CHRISTINE is about to open the dressing room door, she
hears the PHANTOM's voice out of nowhere)*

PHANTOM'S VOICE

Bravi, bravi, bravissimi ...

*(CHRISTINE is bewildered by the voice. MEG,
following, has not heard it. CHRISTINE turns in
surprise, and is relieved to see her)*

MEG

**Where in the world
have you been hiding?
Really, you were
perfect!**

**I only wish
I knew your secret!
Who is this new
tutor!**

CHRISTINE *(abstracted, entering the dressing
room)*

**Father once spoke
of an angel ...
I used to dream he'd
appear ...**

**Now as I sing
I can sense him ...
And I know
he's here ...**

(trance-like)

**Here in this room
he calls me softly ...
somewhere inside ...
hiding ...**

**Somehow I know
he's always with me ...
he – the unseen
genius ...**

MEG *(uneasily)*

**Christine, you must have
been dreaming ...
stories like this can't
come true ...**

**Christine, you're talking
in riddles ...
and it's not
like you ...**

CHRISTINE *(not hearing her, ecstatic)*

**Angel of Music!
Guide
and guardian!
Grant to me your
glory!**

MEG *(to herself)*

**Who is this angel?
This ...**

BOTH

**Angel of Music!
Hide
no longer!
Secret and strange
angel ...**

CHRISTINE *(darkly)*

**He's with me
even now ...**

MEG *(bewildered)*

Your hands are cold ...

CHRISTINE

All around me ...

MEG

**Your face, Christine,
it's white ...**

CHRISTINE

It frightens me ...

MEG

Don't be frightened ...

*(THEY look at each other. The moment is broken by
the arrival of GIRY)*
GIRY
Meg Giry, Are you a dancer? Then come and
practice.
(MEG leaves and joins the DANCERS)
My dear, I was asked to give you this.
*(She hands CHRISTINE a note, and exits.
CHRISTINE opens it and reads)*
CHRISTINE
A red scarf ... the attic ... Little Lotte ...

Scene 3
CHRISTINE'S DRESSING ROOM

*(Meanwhile, RAOUL, ANDRÉ, FIRMIN, and
MME. FIRMIN are seen making their way towards
the dressing room, the MANAGERS in high spirits,
bearing champagne)*
ANDRÉ
A tour de force! No other way to describe it!
FIRMIN
What a relief! Not a single refund!
MME. FIRMIN
Greedy.
ANDRÉ
Richard, I think we've made quite a discovery
in Miss Daaé!
FIRMIN *(to RAOUL, indicating CHRISTINE'S
dressing room)*
Here we are, Monsieur le Vicomte.
RAOUL
Gentlemen, if you wouldn't mind. This is one
visit I should prefer to make unaccompanied.
(He takes the champagne from FIRMIN)
ANDRÉ
As you wish, monsieur.
(They bow and move off)
FIRMIN
They appear to have met before ...
(RAOUL knocks at the door and enters)
RAOUL
Christine Daaé, where is your scarf?
CHRISTINE
Monsieur?
RAOUL
You can't have lost it. After all the trouble I
took. I was just fourteen and soaked to the
skin ...
CHRISTINE
Because you had run into the sea to fetch my
scarf. Oh, Raoul, So it *is* you!
RAOUL
Christine.
*(They embrace and laugh. She moves away and sits at
her dressing table)*

RAOUL

'Little Lotte let her mind wander ...'

CHRISTINE

You remember that, too ...

RAOUL *(continuing)*

**'... Little Lotte thought: Am I fonder of
dolls ...'**

BOTH *(CHRISTINE joining in)*

**'... or of goblins,
of shoes ...'**

CHRISTINE

**'... or of riddles,
of frocks ...'**

RAOUL

Those picnics in the attic ...

'... or of chocolates ...'

CHRISTINE

Father playing the violin ...

RAOUL

As we read to each other dark stories of the
North ...

CHRISTINE
'No— what I love best, Lotte said,
is when I'm asleep in my bed,
and the Angel of Music sings songs in my
head!'

BOTH
'... The Angel of Music sings songs in my
head!'

CHRISTINE *(turning in her chair to look at him)*
Father said, 'When I'm in heaven, child, I
will send the Angel of Music to you'. Well,
father is dead, Raoul, and I *have* been visited
by the Angel of Music.
RAOUL
No doubt of it – And now we'll go to supper!
CHRISTINE
No, Raoul, the Angel of Music is very strict.
RAOUL
I shan't keep you up late!
CHRISTINE
No, Raoul ...
RAOUL
You must change. *I* must get my hat. Two
minutes – Little Lotte.
(He hurries out)
CHRISTINE *(calling after him)*
Raoul!
(quietly picking up her hand mirror)
Things have changed, Raoul.
*(Tremulous music. CHRISTINE hears the
PHANTOM'S voice, seemingly from behind her
dressing room mirror)*

PHANTOM'S VOICE
Insolent boy!
This slave
of fashion
basking in *your*
glory!

Ignorant fool!
This brave
young suitor,
sharing in *my*
triumph!

CHRISTINE *(spell-bound)*
Angel! I hear you!
Speak –
I listen ...
stay by my side,
guide me!

Angel, my soul was
weak –
forgive me ...
enter at last,
Master!

PHANTOM'S VOICE
Flattering child
you shall know me,
see why in shadow
I hide!

Look at your face
in the mirror –
I am there
inside!

*(The figure of the PHANTOM becomes discernible
behind the mirror)*

CHRISTINE *(ecstatic)*
Angel of Music!
Guide
and guardian!
Grant to me your
Glory!

Angel of Music!
Hide
no longer!
Come to me, strange
Angel ...

PHANTOM'S VOICE
I am your Angel ...
Come to me: Angel of Music ...

*(CHRISTINE walks towards the glowing, shimmering
glass. Meanwhile, RAOUL has returned. He hears the
voices and is puzzled. He tries the door. It is locked)*

RAOUL
Whose is that voice ...?
Who *is* that in there ...?

*(Inside the room the mirror opens. Behind it, in an
inferno of white light, stands the PHANTOM. He reaches
forward and takes CHRISTINE firmly, but not fiercely,
by the wrist. His touch is cold, and CHRISTINE gasps)*

PHANTOM
I am your Angel of Music ...
Come to me: Angel of Music ...

*(CHRISTINE disappears through the mirror, which
closes behind her. The door of the dressing room suddenly
unlocks and swings open, and RAOUL enters to find the
room empty)*

RAOUL
Christine! Angel!

Scene 4
THE LABYRINTH UNDERGROUND
*(The PHANTOM and CHRISTINE take their strange
journey to the PHANTOM'S lair.*
*Candles rise from the stage. We see CHRISTINE and
the PHANTOM in a boat which moves slowly across
the misty waters of the underground lake)*

CHRISTINE
In sleep
he sang to me,
in dreams
he came ...
that voice
which calls to me
and speaks
my name ...

And do
I dream again?
For now
I find
the Phantom of the Opera
is there –
inside my mind ...

PHANTOM
Sing once
again with me
our strange
duet ...
My power
over you
grows stronger
yet ...

And though
you turn from me,
to glance
behind,
the Phantom of the Opera
is there –
inside your mind ...

CHRISTINE
Those who
have seen your face
draw back
in fear ...
I am
the mask you wear ...

PHANTOM
It's me
they hear ...

BOTH

Your/my spirit
and your/my voice
in one
combined:
the Phantom of the Opera
is there –
inside your/my mind ...

OFFSTAGE VOICES

He's there,
the Phantom of the Opera ...
Beware
the Phantom of the Opera ...

PHANTOM

In all
your fantasies,
you always
knew
that man
and mystery ...

CHRISTINE

... were both
in you ...

BOTH

And in
this labyrinth
where night
is blind,
the Phantom of the Opera
is there/here –
inside your/my mind ...

PHANTOM

Sing, my Angel of Music!

CHRISTINE

He's there
the Phantom of the Opera ...

(She begins to vocalize strangely, her song becoming more and more extravagant.)

Scene 5

BEYOND THE LAKE, THE NEXT MORNING

*(Finally they arrive in the PHANTOM'S lair.
Downstage, the candles in the lake lift up revealing
giant candelabra outlining the space.
The boat turns into a bed, there is a huge pipe organ.
The PHANTOM sits at the organ and takes over the
accompaniment)*

PHANTOM

I have brought you
to the seat of sweet
music's throne ...
to this kingdom
where all must pay
homage to music ...
music ...

You have come here,
for one purpose,
and one alone ...
Since the moment
I first heard you sing,
I have needed
you with me,
to serve me, to sing,
for my music ...
my music ...

(changing mood)

Night-time sharpens,
heightens each sensation ...
Darkness stirs and
wakes imagination ...
Silently the senses
abandon their defences ...

Slowly, gently
night unfurls its splendour ...
Grasp it, sense it –
tremulous and tender ...
Turn your face away
from the garish light of day,
turn your thoughts away
from cold, unfeeling light –
and listen to
the music of the night ...

Close your eyes
and surrender to your
darkest dreams!
Purge your thoughts
of the life
you knew before!
Close your eyes,
let your spirit
start to soar!
And you'll live
as you've never
lived before ...

Softly, deftly,
music shall surround you ...
Feel it, hear it,
closing in around you ...
Open up your mind,
let your fantasies unwind,
in this darkness which
you know you cannot fight –
the darkness of
the music of the night.

Let your mind
start a journey through a
strange, new world!
Leave all thoughts
of the world
you knew before!
Let your soul
Take you where you
long to be!
Only then
can you belong
to me ...

Floating, falling,
sweet intoxication!
Touch me, trust me,
savour each sensation!
Let the dream begin,
let your darker side give in
to the power of
the music that I write –
the power of
the music of the night ...

During all this, the PHANTOM has conditioned CHRISTINE to the coldness of his touch and her fingers are brave enough to stray to his mask and caress it, with no hint of removing it. The PHANTOM leads her to a large mirror from which he removes a dustcover and in which we see the image of CHRISTINE, a perfect wax-face impression, wearing a wedding gown. CHRISTINE moves slowly towards it, when suddenly the image thrusts its hands through the mirror towards her. She faints. The PHANTOM catches her and carries her to the bed, where he lays her down)

PHANTOM
You alone
can make my song take flight –
help me make the music of the night …

Scene 6
THE NEXT MORNING

(As the light brightens, we see the PHANTOM seated at the organ, playing with furious concentration. He breaks off occasionally to write the music down. There is a musical box, in the shape of a barrel organ beside the bed. Mysteriously, it plays as CHRISTINE wakes up. The music keeps her in a half-trance)

CHRISTINE
I remember
there was mist …
swirling mist
upon a vast, glassy lake …

There were candles
all around,
and on the lake there
was a boat,
and in the boat
there was a man …

(She rises and approaches the PHANTOM, who does not see her. As she reaches for his mask, he turns, almost catching her. This happens several times)

Who was that shape
in the shadows?
Whose is the face
in the mask?

(She finally succeeds in tearing the mask from his face. The PHANTOM springs up and rounds on her furiously. She clearly sees his face. The audience does not, as he is standing in profile and in shadow)

PHANTOM
Damn you!
You little prying
Pandora!
You little demon –
is this what you wanted to see?

Curse you!
You little lying
Delilah!
You little viper –
now you cannot ever be free!

Damn you …
Curse you …

(a pause)

Stranger
than you dreamt it –
can you even
dare to look
or bear to
think of me:
this loathsome
gargoyle, who
burns in hell, but secretly
yearns for heaven,
secretly …
secretly …

But, Christine …

Fear can
Turn to love – you'll
learn to see, to
find the man
behind the
monster: this …
repulsive
carcass, who
seems a beast, but secretly
dreams of beauty,
secretly …
secretly …

Oh, Christine …

(He holds out his hand for the mask, which she gives to him. He puts it on, turning towards the audience as he sings):

Come we must return –
those two fools
who run my theatre
will be missing you.

(The lair sinks into the floor as the PHANTOM and CHRISTINE leave)

Scene 7
BACKSTAGE

(BUQUET mysteriously appears, a length of fabric serving as a cloak, and a piece of rope as the Punjab lasso. He is showing off to the BALLET GIRLS)

BUQUET
Like yellow parchment
is his skin …
a great black hole served as the
nose that never grew …

(Demonstrating his method of self-defence against the Punjab lasso, he inserts his hand between his neck and the noose, and then pulls the rope taut. With a mixture of horror and delight, the BALLET GIRLS applaud this demonstration)

(explaining to them)
You must be always
on your guard,
or he will catch you with his
magical lasso!

(A trap opens up centre stage, casting a shadow of the PHANTOM as he emerges. The GIRLS, linking hands, run off terrified. The PHANTOM, leading CHRISTINE, fixes his stare on BUQUET. Sweeping his cape around CHRISTINE, he exits with her. But before they go, GIRY has entered, observing. She turns on BUQUET)

GIRY
Those who speak
of what they know
find, too late, that prudent
silence is wise.

Joseph Buquet,
hold your tongue –
he will burn you with the
heat of his eyes ...

Scene 8
THE MANAGERS' OFFICE

(Desk, chairs, papers. FIRMIN is scornfully eyeing a newspaper article)

FIRMIN
'Mystery
after gala night,'
it says, 'Mystery
of soprano's flight!'

'Mystified,
baffled Sûreté say,
we are mystified –
we suspect foul play!'

(He lowers the paper)

Bad news on
soprano scene –
first Carlotta,
now Christine!
Still, at least
The seats get sold –
gossip's worth
its weight in gold ...

What a way to
run a business!
Spare me these
unending trials!
Half your cast disappears,
but the crowd still cheers!
Opera!
To hell with Gluck and Handel –
It's a scandal that'll
pack 'em in the aisles!

(ANDRÉ bursts in, in a temper)

ANDRÉ
Damnable!
Will they all walk out?
This is damnable!

FIRMIN
André, please don't shout ...

It's publicity!
And the take is vast!
Free publicity!

ANDRÉ
But we have no cast ...

FIRMIN *(calmly)*
But André,
have you seen the queue?

(He has been sorting mail on his desk. Finding the two letters from the PHANTOM):

Oh, it seems
you've got one too ...

(He hands the letter to ANDRÉ, who opens it and reads):

ANDRÉ
'Dear André
what a charming gala!
Christine enjoyed a great success!
We were hardly bereft
when Carlotta left –
otherwise,
the chorus was entrancing,
but the dancing was a
lamentable mess!'

FERMIN *(reading his)*
'Dear Firmin,
just a brief reminder:
my salary has not been paid.
Send it care of the ghost,
by return of post –
P.T.O.:
No one likes a debtor,
so it's better if my
orders are obeyed!'

FIRMIN/ANDRÉ
Who would have the gall
to send this?
Someone with a puerile brain!

FIRMIN *(examining both letters)*
These are both signed 'O.G.' ...

ANDRÉ
Who the hell is he?

BOTH *(immediately realizing)*
Opera ghost!

FIRMIN *(unamused)*
It's really not amusing!

ANDRÉ
He's abusing
our position!

FIRMIN
In addition
he wants money!

ANDRÉ
He's a funny
sort of spectre ...

BOTH
... to expect a
large retainer!
Nothing plainer –
he is clearly quite insane!

(They are interrupted by the arrival of RAOUL, who brandishes another of the PHANTOM'S notes)

RAOUL
Where is she?

ANDRÉ
You mean Carlotta?

RAOUL
I mean Miss Daaé –
where is she?

FIRMIN
Well, how should we know?

RAOUL
I want an answer –
I take it that you
sent me this note?

FIRMIN
What's all this nonsense?

ANDRÉ
Of course not!

FIRMIN
Don't look at us!

RAOUL
She's not with you, then?

FIRMIN
Of course not!

ANDRÉ
We're in the dark ...

RAOUL
Monsieur, don't argue –
Isn't this the
letter you wrote?

FIRMIN
And what is it, that we're
meant to have wrote?

(Realizing his mistake)
Written!

(RAOUL hands the note to ANDRÉ, who reads it)

ANDRÉ
'Do not fear for Miss Daaé.
The Angel of Music
has her under his wing.
make no attempt to see her again.'

(The MANAGERS look mystified)

RAOUL
If you didn't write it, who did?

(CARLOTTA bursts in. She too has a letter, which has cheered her no more than the others)

CARLOTTA
Where is he?

ANDRÉ
Ah, welcome back!

CARLOTTA
Your precious patron –
where is he?

RAOUL
What is it now?

CARLOTTA *(to RAOUL)*
I have your letter –
a letter which I
rather resent!

FIRMIN *(to RAOUL)*
And did you send it?

RAOUL
Of course not!

ANDRÉ
As if he would!

CARLOTTA
You didn't send it?

RAOUL
Of course not!

FIRMIN
What's going on ...?

CARLOTTA *(to RAOUL)*
You dare to tell me,
that this is not the
letter you sent?!

RAOUL
And what is it that I'm
meant to have sent?

(RAOUL takes the letter and reads it)
'Your days
at the Opéra Populaire are numbered.
Christine Daaé
will be singing on your behalf tonight.
Be prepared
for a great misfortune,
should you attempt
to take her place.'

(The MANAGERS are beginning to tire of the intrigue)

ANDRÉ/FERMIN
Far too many
notes for *my* taste -
and most of them
about Christine!
All we've heard since we came
is Miss Daaé's name ...

(GIRY suddenly appears, accompanied by MEG)

GIRY
Miss Daaé has returned.

FIRMIN *(dryly)*
I trust her midnight oil
is well and truly burned.

ANDRÉ
Where precisely is she now?

GIRY
I thought it best
that she went home ...

MEG
She needed rest.

RAOUL
May I see her?

GIRY
No, monsieur,
she will see no one.

CARLOTTA
Will she sing?
Will she sing?

GIRY
Here, I have a note ...

RAOUL/CARLOTTA/ANDRÉ
Let me see it!

FIRMIN *(snatching it)*
Please!

FIRMIN *(Opens the letter and reads. The PHANTOM'S voice gradually takes over)*
'Gentlemen, I have now sent you several notes of the most amiable nature, detailing how my theatre is to be run. You have not followed my instructions. I shall give you one last chance ...'

PHANTOM'S VOICE *(taking over)*
Christine Daaé has returned to you,
and I am anxious her career
should progress.
In the new production of 'Il Muto',
you will therefore cast Carlotta
as the Pageboy, and put Miss Daaé
in the rôle of Countess.
The rôle which Miss Daaé plays
calls for charm and appeal.
The rôle of the Pageboy is silent –
which makes my casting,
in a word, ideal.

I shall watch the performance from my normal seat in Box Five, which will be kept empty for me. Should these commands be ignored, a disaster beyond your imagination will occur.

FIRMIN *(taking over)*
'I remain Gentlemen,
Your obedient servant, O.G.'

CARLOTTA
Christine!

ANDRÉ
Whatever next ...?

CARLOTTA
It's all a ploy to
help Christine!

FIRMIN
This is insane ...

CARLOTTA
I know who sent this:
(Pointing an accusing finger)
The Vicomte – her lover!

RAOUL *(ironical)*
Indeed? *(to the OTHERS)*
Can you believe this?

ANDRÉ *(to CARLOTTA, in protest)*
Signora!

CARLOTTA *(half to the MANAGERS, half to herself)*
O traditori!

FIRMIN *(to CARLOTTA)*
This is a joke!

ANDRÉ
This changes nothing!

CARLOTTA
O mentitori!

FIRMIN
Signora!

ANDRÉ
You are our star!

FIRMIN
And always will be!

ANDRÉ
Signora ...

FIRMIN
The man is mad!

ANDRÉ
We don't take orders!

FIRMIN *(announcing it to EVERYONE)*
Miss Daaé will be playing
the Pageboy – the silent rôle ...

ANDRÉ/FIRMIN
Carlotta will be playing
the lead!

CARLOTTA *(waxing melodramatic)*
It's useless trying to
appease me!
You're only saying this
to please me!
Signori, è vero?
Non, non, non voglio udire!
Lasciatemi morire!
O padre mio!
Dio!

GIRY
Who scorn his word,
beware to those ...

CARLOTTA *(to MANAGERS)*
You have reviled me!

GIRY
The angel sees,
the angel knows ...

RAOUL
Why did Christine
fly from my arms ...?

CARLOTTA
You have rebuked me!

ANDRÉ/FIRMIN
Signora, pardon us ...

CARLOTTA
You have replaced me!

ANDRÉ/FIRMIN
Please, Signora
we beseech you ...

GIRY
This hour shall see
your darkest fears ...

MEG/RAOUL
I must see her ...

CARLOTTA
Abbandonata!
Deseredata!
O, sventurata!

GIRY
The angel knows,
the angel hears ...

RAOUL
Where did she go ...?

CARLOTTA
Abbandonata!
Disgraziata!

ANDRÉ/FIRMIN
Signora, sing for us!
Don't be a martyr ...

RAOUL/GIRY/MEG
What new surprises
lie in store ...?

ANDRÉ/FIRMIN
Our star ...!

CARLOTTA
Non vo' cantar!

(ALL look at CARLOTTA, as the MANAGERS approach
her lovingly)

ANDRÉ
Your public needs you!

FIRMIN
We need you, too!

CARLOTTA (unassauged)
Would you not
rather have your
precious little
ingenue?

ANDRÉ/FIRMIN
Signora, no!
the world wants *you!*

(The MANAGERS adopt their most persuasive attitudes)

ANDRÉ/FIRMIN
Prima donna,
first lady of the stage!
Your devotees
are on their knees
to implore you!

ANDRÉ
Can you bow out
when they're shouting
your name?

FIRMIN
Think of how they all
adore you!

BOTH
Prima donna,
enchant us once again!

ANDRÉ
Think of your muse ...

FIRMIN
And of the queues
round the theatre!

BOTH
Can you deny
us the triumph
in store?
Sing, prima donna,
once more!

(CARLOTTA registers her acceptance, as the
MANAGERS continue to cajole and the OTHERS reflect
variously on the situation)

RAOUL
Christine spoke of an angel ...

CARLOTTA (to herself, in triumph)
Prima donna,
your song shall live again!

ANDRÉ/FIRMIN (to CARLOTTA)
Think of your public!

CARLOTTA
You took a snub
but there's a public
who needs you!

GIRY (referring to CHRISTINE)
She has heard the voice
of the angel of music ...

ANDRÉ/FIRMIN (to CARLOTTA)
Those who hear your voice
liken you to an angel!

CARLOTTA
Think of their cry
of undying
support!

RAOUL
Is this her angel of music ...?

ANDRÉ (to FIRMIN)
We get our opera ...

FIRMIN (to ANDRÉ)
She gets her limelight!

CARLOTTA
Follow where the limelight
leads you!

MEG
Is this ghost
an angel or a madman ...?

RAOUL
Angel or madman ...?

ANDRÉ/FIRMIN (aside)
Leading ladies are a trial!

CARLOTTA
Prima donna,
your song shall never die!

MEG
Voice of hell, or of heaven ...?

GIRY
Heaven help you,
those who doubt ...

CARLOTTA
You'll sing again,
and to unending
ovation!

RAOUL
Orders! Warnings!
Lunatic demands!

GIRY
This miscasting
will invite damnation ...

ANDRÉ/FIRMIN
Tears ... oaths ...
lunatic demands
are regular occurrences!

MEG
Bliss or damnation?
Which has claimed her ...?

CARLOTTA
Think how you'll shine
in that final
encore!
Sing, prima donna,
once more!

GIRY
Oh fools,
to have flouted his warnings!

RAOUL
Surely, for her sake ...

MEG
Surely he'll strike back ...

ANDRÉ/FIRMIN
Surely there'll be further scenes –
worse than this!

GIRY
Think, before
these demands are rejected!

RAOUL
... I must see
these demands are rejected!

MEG
... if his threats
and demands are rejected!

ANDRÉ/FIRMIN
Who'd believe a diva
happy to relieve a
chorus girl, who's gone
and slept with the patron?
Raoul and the soubrette,
entwined in love's duet!
Although he may demur,
he must have been with her!

MEG/RAOUL
Christine must be protected!

CARLOTTA
O, fortunata!
Non ancor
abbandonata!

ANDRÉ/FIRMIN
You'd never get away
with all this in a play,
but if it's loudly sung
and in a foreign tongue,
it's just the sort of story
audiences adore, in
fact a perfect
opera!

RAOUL
His game is over!

GIRY
This is a game
you cannot hope to win!

RAOUL
And in Box Five
a new game will begin . . .

GIRY
For, if his curse
is on this opera . . .

MEG
But if his curse
is on this opera . . .

ANDRÉ/FIRMIN
Prima donna,
the world is at your feet!
A nation waits,
and how it hates
to be cheated!

CARLOTTA
The stress that falls upon a
famous prima donna!
Terrible diseases,
coughs and colds and sneezes!
Still, the dryest throat
will reach the highest note,
in search of perfect
opera!

MEG/GIRY
. . . then I fear the outcome . . .

RAOUL
Christine plays the Pageboy,
Carlotta plays the Countess . . .

GIRY
. . . should you dare to . . .

MEG
. . . when you once again . . .

ALL
Light up the stage
with that age-old
rapport!
Sing, prima donna,
once more!

PHANTOM'S VOICE
So, it is to be war between us! If these
demands are not met, a disaster beyond your
imagination will occur!

ALL
Once more!

Scene 9
A PERFORMANCE OF 'IL MUTO' BY ALBRIZZIO

*(During the overture RAOUL, ANDRÉ and FIRMIN
take their respective seats – RAOUL in Box Five, the
MANAGERS in a box opposite)*

RAOUL
Gentlemen, if you would care to take your
seats? I shall be sitting in Box Five.

ANDRÉ
Do you really think that's wise, monsieur?

RAOUL
My dear André, there would appear to be no
seats available, other than Box Five . . .

*(The front cloth rises to reveal an 18th Century salon,
a canopied bed centre-stage. The COUNTESS is
played by CARLOTTA, SERAFIMO, the page boy, is
disguised as her maid and is played by CHRISTINE.
At this point they are hidden behind the drapes of the
bed, which are drawn.*

*In the room are TWO EPICENE MEN: one a
HAIRDRESSER and one a JEWELLER. The
JEWELLER is attended by MEG. There is also an
OLDER WOMAN, the COUNTESS' confidante. All
apart from MEG are gossiping with relish about the
COUNTESS' current liaison with SERAFIMO)*

> CONFIDANTE
> They say that this youth
> has set my Lady's
> heart aflame!
> 1ST FOP
> His Lordship, sure,
> would die of shock!
> 2ND FOP
> His Lordship is
> a laughing-stock!
> CONFIDANTE
> Should he suspect her,
> God protect her!
> ALL THREE
> Shame! Shame! Shame!
> This faithless lady's
> bound for Hades!
> Shame! Shame! Shame!

*(The canopy drapes part and we see the COUNTESS
kissing SERAFIMO passionately. As the recitative
begins, the lights and music dim on stage, and our
attention turns to the MANAGERS in their box)*

IN THE BOX
ANDRÉ
Nothing like the old operas!

FIRMIN
Or the old scenery . . .
ANDRÉ
The old singers . . .
FIRMIN
The old audience . . .
ANDRÉ
And every seat sold!
FIRMIN
Hardly a disaster beyond all imagination!
*(They chuckle, and nod to RAOUL in the opposite
box. He acknowledges them)*
ON STAGE
COUNTESS
Serafimo – your disguise is perfect.
(A knock at the door)
Who can this be?
DON ATTILIO
Gentle wife, admit your loving
husband.
ATTENTION BACK ON STAGE
*(The COUNTESS admits DON ATTILIO. He is an
old fool)*
DON ATTILIO
My love – I am called to England
on affairs of State, and must
leave you with your new maid.
(Aside) Though I'd happily take
the maid with me.
COUNTESS *(aside)*
The old fool's leaving!
DON ATTILIO *(aside)*
I suspect my young bride is untrue to me. I
shall not leave, but hide over there to observe
her!
DON ATTILIO *(to COUNTESS)*
Addio!
COUNTESS
Addio!
BOTH *(to each other)*
Addio!
*He goes, pretending to leave, then hides and watches
the action)*

COUNTESS *(CARLOTTA)*
Serafimo – away with this pretence!

*(She rips off SERAFIMO'S skirt to reveal his manly
breeches)*

**You cannot speak, but kiss me in my
husband's absence!**

**Poor fool, he makes me laugh!
Haha,
Haha! etc.
Time I tried to get a better better half!**

COUNTESS AND CHORUS
**Poor fool, he doesn't know!
Hoho,
Hoho, etc.
If he knew the truth, he'd never, ever go!**

(Suddenly from nowhere, we hear the voice of the PHANTOM)

PHANTOM'S VOICE

Did I not instruct that Box Five was to be kept empty?

> MEG *(terrified)*
> He's here: the Phantom of the Opera . . .
> *(General reaction of bewilderment. CHRISTINE looks fearfully about her)*

CHRISTINE

It's him . . . I know it . . . it's him . . .

CARLOTTA *(Finding a scapegoat in CHRISTINE, hisses at her)*

Your part is silent, little toad!

(But the PHANTOM has heard her)

PHANTOM'S VOICE

A toad, madame? Perhaps it is *you* who are the toad . . .

(Again unease. CARLOTTA and the CONDUCTOR confer and pick up the opening of the scene)

CARLOTTA *(As the COUNTESS)*

Serafimo, away with this pretence!
You cannot speak, but kiss me in my
croak!

(Instead of singing, she emits a great croak, like a toad. A stunned silence. CARLOTTA is as amazed as anyone, but regains herself and continues. More perturbing, however, is a new sound: the PHANTOM is laughing – quietly at first, then more and more hysterically)

CARLOTTA *(as the COUNTESS)*

Poor fool, he makes me laugh –
Hahahahaha!
Croak, croak, croak,
croak, croak, croak, etc.

(As before. The PHANTOM'S laughter rises. The croaking continues as the chandelier's lights blink on and off. The PHANTOM'S laughter, by this time overpowering, now crescendos into a great cry):

PHANTOM'S VOICE

Behold! She is singing to bring down the chandelier!

(CARLOTTA looks tearfully up at the MANAGERS' box and shakes her head)

CARLOTTA

Non posso più . . .
I cannot . . . I cannot go on . . .

PIANGI *(rushing on)*

Cara, cara . . . I'm here . . .
is all right . . . Come . . . I'm here . . .

(ANDRÉ and FIRMIN hurry out of the box onto the stage. PIANGI ushers the now sobbing CARLOTTA offstage, while the MANAGERS tackle the audience)

FIRMIN

Ladies and gentlemen, the performance will continue in ten minutes' time . . .

(He addresses Box Five, keeping one eye on the chandelier as it returns to normal)

. . . when the rôle of the Countess will be sung by Miss Christine Daaé.

ANDRÉ *(improvising)*

In the meantime, ladies and gentlemen, we shall be giving you the ballet from Act Three of tonight's opera.

(to the CONDUCTOR)

Maestro – the ballet – now!

(The MANAGERS leave, the stage is cleared and music starts again.
The BALLET GIRLS enter, as a sylvan glade flies in. They begin the Dance of the Country Nymphs. Upstage, behind the drop, a series of threatening shadows of the PHANTOM. MEG is aware of them and dances out of step. When this culminates in one gigantic, oppressive, bat-like shadow, the garrotted body of JOSEPH BUQUET falls onto the stage, causing the sylvan glade to fly out. Pandemonium)

CHRISTINE *(calling for help)*

Raoul! Raoul!

(RAOUL runs on stage and embraces her)

RAOUL *(to CHRISTINE, leading her away)*

Christine, come with me . .

CHRISTINE

No . . . to the roof. We'll be safe there.

(CHRISTINE and RAOUL hurry off)

FIRMIN *(Attempting to placate the audience, as STAGE-HANDS and POLICEMEN crowd onto the stage)*

Ladies and gentlemen, please remain in your seats. Do not panic. It was an accident . . . simply an accident . . .

Scene 10

THE ROOF OF THE OPERA HOUSE

(A statue of 'La Victoire Ailée' – the same as that which tops the proscenium. It is twilight. CHRISTINE and RAOUL rush on)

RAOUL

Why have you brought us here?

CHRISTINE

Don't take me back there!

RAOUL

We must return!

CHRISTINE

He'll kill me!

RAOUL

Be still now . . .

CHRISTINE

His eyes will find me there!

RAOUL

Christine, don't say that . . .

CHRISTINE

Those eyes that burn!

RAOUL

Don't even think it . . .

CHRISTINE

And if he has to kill
a thousand men –

RAOUL

Forget this waking nightmare . . .

CHRISTINE

The Phantom of the Opera will kill . . .

RAOUL

This phantom is a fable . . .
Believe me . . .

CHRISTINE

. . . and kill again!

RAOUL

There is no Phantom of the Opera . . .

CHRISTINE

My God, who is this man . . .

RAOUL

My God, who is this man . . .

CHRISTINE

. . . who hunts to kill . . .?

RAOUL

. . . this mask of death . . .?

CHRISTINE

I can't escape from him . . .

RAOUL

Whose is this voice you hear . . .

CHRISTINE

. . . I never will!

RAOUL

. . . with every breath . . .?

BOTH

And in this
labyrinth
where night is blind,
the Phantom of the Opera
is here:
inside your/my mind . . .

RAOUL

There is no Phantom of the Opera . . .

CHRISTINE

Raoul, I've been there –
to his world of
unending night . . .
To a world where
the daylight dissolves
into darkness . . .
darkness . . .

Raoul, I've seen him!
Can I ever
forget that sight?
Can I ever
escape from that face?
So distorted,
deformed, it
was hardly a face,
in that darkness . . .
darkness . . .

(trancelike, then becoming more and more ecstatic)

But his voice
filled my spirit
with a strange, sweet sound . . .
In that night
there was music
in my mind . . .
And through music
my soul began
to soar!
And I heard
as I'd never
heard before . . .

RAOUL

What you heard
was a dream
and nothing more . . .

CHRISTINE

Yet in his eyes
all the sadness
of the world . . .
Those pleading eyes,
that both threaten
and adore . . .

RAOUL *(comforting)*

Christine . . .
Christine . . .

PHANTOM *(unseen, a ghostly echo of RAOUL'S words)*

Christine . . .

CHRISTINE

What was that?

(A moment, as their eyes meet. The mood changes)

RAOUL

No more talk
of darkness,
Forget these
wide-eyed fears.
I'm here,
nothing can harm you –
my words will
warm and calm you.

Let me be
your freedom,
let daylight
dry your tears.
I'm here,
with you, beside you,
to guard you
and to guide you . . .

CHRISTINE

Say you love me
every
waking moment,
turn my head
with talk of summertime . . .

Anywhere you go
let me go to . . .
Love me –
that's all I ask
of you . . .

Say you need me
with you,
now and always ...
promise me that all
you say is true –
that's all I ask
of you ...

RAOUL

Let me be
your shelter,
let me
be your light.
You're safe:
No one will find you –
your fears are
far behind you ...

CHRISTINE

All I want
is freedom,
a world with
no more night ...
and you,
always beside me,
to hold me
and to hide me ...

RAOUL

Then say you'll share with
me one
love, one lifetime ...
let me lead you
from your solitude ...

Say you need me
with you
here, beside you ...
anywhere you go,
let me go too –
Christine,
that's all I ask
of you ...

CHRISTINE

Say you'll share with
me one
love, one lifetime ...
say the word
and I will follow you ...

BOTH

Share each day with
me, each
night, each morning ...

CHRISTINE

Say you love me ...

RAOUL

You know I do ...

BOTH

Love me –
that's all I ask
of you ...

(They kiss)

Anywhere you go
let me go too ...
Love me –
that's all I ask
of you ...

(CHRISTINE starts from her reverie)

CHRISTINE

I must go –
they'll wonder
where I am ...
wait for me, Raoul!

RAOUL

Christine, I love you!

CHRISTINE

Order your
fine horses!
Be with them
at the door!

RAOUL

And soon you'll be beside me!

CHRISTINE

You'll guard me, and you'll guide me ...

(They hurry off. The PHANTOM emerges from behind the statue)

PHANTOM

I gave you my music ...
made your song take wing ...
and now, how you've
repaid me:
denied me
and betrayed me ...
He was bound to love you
when he heard you sing ...

Christine ...
Christine ...

RAOUL/CHRISTINE *(offstage)*

Say you'll share with
me one
love, one lifetime ...
say the word
and I will follow you ...

Share each day with
me, each
night, each morning ...

PHANTOM

You will curse the day
you did not do
all that the Phantom asked
of you ...!

(As the roof of the opera house disappears, the opera curtain closes and the PRINCIPALS in 'Il Muto' appear through it for their bows, CHRISTINE conspicuously dressed in CARLOTTA'S costume. Simultaneously, we hear the maniacal laughter of the PHANTOM and we see him high above the stage, perilously rocking the chandelier. The lights of the chandelier begin flickering and, at a great cry from him, it descends, swinging more and more madly over the orchestra pit)

PHANTOM

Go!!

(The chandelier falls to the stage at CHRISTINE'S feet)

END OF ACT ONE

Scene 1
THE STAIRCASE OF THE OPÉRA HOUSE

(A gauze half conceals the tableau of guests at the opera ball. The guests (whom we cannot yet see clearly) are in fancy dress – a peacock, a lion, a dragon, Mephistopheles, a highwayman, a clown, knights, ladies, an executioner. M. ANDRÉ enters. He is dressed as a skeleton, in an opera cape. Almost immediately M. FIRMIN arrives. He is also dressed as a skeleton in an opera cape. The two skeletons see each other and approach nervously)

ANDRÉ
M'sieur Firmin?

FIRMIN
M'sieur André?

(Each raises his mask to the other. They recognize each other)

FIRMIN
**Dear André,
what a splendid party!**

ANDRÉ
**The prologue
to a bright new year!**

FIRMIN
**Quite a night!
I'm impressed!**

FIRMIN
**Well, one does
one's best ...**

ANDRÉ/FIRMIN *(raising their glasses)*
Here's to us!

FIRMIN
**I must say
all the same, that
it's a shame that 'Phantom'
fellow isn't here!**

(The gauze lifts fully to reveal the staircase of the opera house. The opera ball begins. Among the GUESTS are four carrying strange percussion instruments: a monkey with cymbals, a toy soldier with a drum, a triangle, bells. Together they play wierdly throughout)

CHORUS
**Masquerade!
Paper faces on parade ...
Masquerade!
Hide your face,
so the world will
never find you!**

**Masquerade!
Every face a different shade ...
Masquerade!
Look around –
there's another
mask behind you!**

**Flash of mauve ...
Splash of puce ...
Fool and king ...
Ghoul and goose ...
Green and black ...
Queen and priest ...
Trace of rouge ...
Face of beast ...**

**Faces ...
Take your turn, take a ride
on the merry-go-round ...
in an inhuman race ...**

**Eye of gold ...
Thigh of blue ...
True is false ...
Who is who ...?
Curl of lip ...
Swirl of gown ...
Ace of hearts ...
Face of clown ...**

**Faces ...
Drink it in, drink it up,
till you've drowned
in the light ...
in the sound ...**

RAOUL/CHRISTINE
But who can name the face ...?

ALL
**Masquerade!
Grinning yellows,
spinning reds ...
Masquerade!
Take your fill –
let the spectacle
astound you!**

**Masquerade!
Burning glances,
turning heads ...
Masquerade!
Stop and stare
at the sea of smiles
around you!**

**Masquerade!
Seething shadows,
breathing lies ...
Masquerade!
You can fool
any friend who
ever knew you!**

**Masquerade!
Leering satyrs,
peering eyes ...
Masquerade!
Run and hide –
but a face will
still pursue you!**

(The ENSEMBLE activity becomes background, as ANDRÉ, FIRMIN, MEG, GIRY, PIANGI and CARLOTTA come to the fore, glasses in hand)

GIRY
What a night!

MEG
What a crowd!

ANDRÉ
Makes you glad!

FIRMIN
**Makes you proud!
All the crème
de la crème!**

CARLOTTA
Watching us watching them!

MEG/GIRY
**And all our fears
are in the past!**

ANDRÉ
Six months ...

PIANGI
Of relief!

CARLOTTA
Of delight!

ANDRÉ/FIRMIN
Of Elysian peace!

MEG/GIRY
And we can breathe at last!

CARLOTTA
No more notes!

PIANGI
No more ghost!

GIRY
Here's a health!

ANDRÉ
**Here's a toast:
to a prosperous year!**

FIRMIN
To the new chandelier!

PIANGI/CARLOTTA
**And may its
splendour never fade!**

FIRMIN
Six months!

GIRY
What a joy!

MEG
What a change!

FIRMIN/ANDRÉ
What a blessed release!

ANDRÉ
And what a masquerade!

(They clink glasses and move off. RAOUL and CHRISTINE emerge. She is admiring a new acquisition: an engagement ring from RAOUL, which she has attached to a gold chain around her neck)

CHRISTINE
Think of it!
A secret engagement!
Look – your future bride!
Just think of it!

RAOUL
But why is it secret?
What have we to hide?

CHRISTINE
Please, let's not fight ...

RAOUL
Christine, you're free!

CHRISTINE
Wait till the time is right ...

RAOUL
When will that be?
It's an engagement,
not a crime!

Christine,
What are you
afraid of?

CHRISTINE
Let's not argue ...

RAOUL
Let's not argue ...

CHRISTINE
Please pretend ...

RAOUL
I can only hope I'll ...

CHRISTINE
You will ...

BOTH
... understand
in time ...

(Dance section, in which CHRISTINE, almost coquettish, almost jittery, goes from man to man. But too many of her partners seem to be replicas of the PHANTOM, and each spins her with increasing force. Eventually RAOUL rescues her and holds her tightly. He whirls her back into the dance, as the music heads towards its climax)

ALL
Masquerade!
Paper faces on parade!
Masquerade!
Hide your face,
so the world will
never find you!

Masquerade!
Every face a different shade!
Masquerade!
Look around –
There's another
mask behind you!

Masquerade!
Burning glances,
turning heads ...
Masquerade!
Stop and stare
at the sea of smiles
around you!

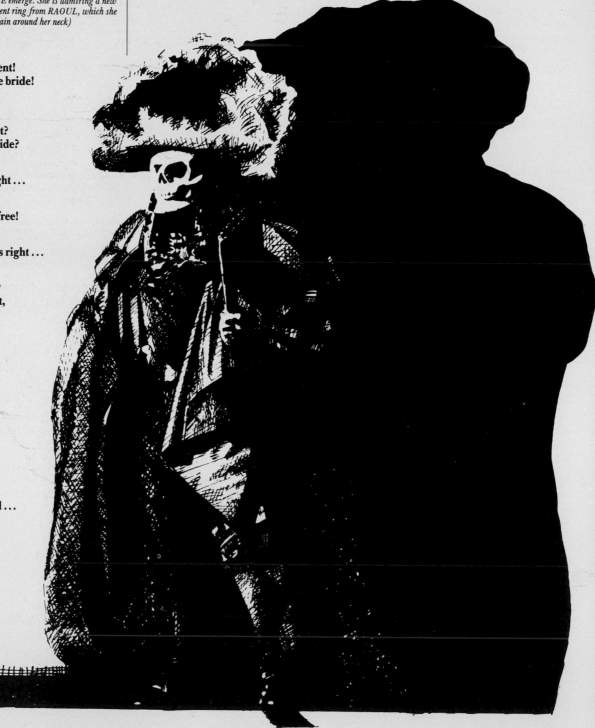

**Masquerade!
Grinning yellows,
spinning reds ...
Masquerade!
Take your fill –
let the spectacle
astound you!**

(At the height of the activity a grotesque figure suddenly appears at the top of the staircase. Dressed all in crimson, with a death's head visible inside the hood of his robe, the PHANTOM has come to the party. With dreadful wooden steps he descends the stairs and takes the centre of the stage)

PHANTOM

**Why so silent, good messieurs?
Did you think that I had left you for good?
Have you missed me, good messieurs?
I have written you an opera!**

(He takes from under his robe an enormous bound manuscript)

**Here I bring the finished score –
'Don Juan Triumphant'!**

(He throws it to ANDRÉ)

**I advise you
to comply –
my instructions
should be clear –
Remember,
there are worse things
than a shattered chandelier ...**

(CHRISTINE, mesmerized, approaches as the PHANTOM beckons her. He reaches out, grasps the chain that holds the secret engagement ring, and rips it from her throat)

**Your chains are still mine –
you will sing for me!**

(ALL cower in suspense as the music crescendos, until, suddenly, his figure evaporates)

Scene 2
BACKSTAGE

(GIRY is hurrying across. RAOUL appears and calls after HER)

RAOUL
Madame Giry. Madame Giry ...

GIRY
Monsieur, don't ask me – I know no more than anyone else.

(She moves off again. He stops her)

RAOUL
That's not true. You've seen something, haven't you?

GIRY *(uneasily)*
I don't know what I've seen ... Please don't ask me, monsieur ...

RAOUL *(desperately)*
Madame, for all our sakes ...

GIRY *(she has glanced nervously about her and, suddenly deciding to trust him, cuts in):*
Very well. It was years ago. There was a travelling fair in the city. Tumblers, conjurors, human oddities ...

RAOUL
Go on ...

GIRY *(trance-like as she retraces the past)*
And there was ... I shall never forget him: a man ... locked in a cage ...

RAOUL
In a *cage* ...?

GIRY
A prodigy, monsieur! Scholar, architect, musician ...

RAOUL *(piecing together the jigsaw)*
A composer ...

GIRY
And an inventor, too, monsieur. They boasted he had once built for the Shah of Persia, a maze of mirrors ...

RAOUL *(mystified and impatient, cuts in)*
Who *was* this man ...?

GIRY *(with a shudder)*
A freak of nature ...
more monster
than man ...

RAOUL *(a murmur)*
Deformed ...?

GIRY
From birth, it seemed ...

RAOUL
My God ...

GIRY
And then ... he went missing. He escaped.

RAOUL
Go on.

GIRY
They never found him –
it was said he
had died ...

RAOUL *(darkly)*
Be he didn't die, did he?

GIRY
The world forgot him,
but I never can ...
For in this darkness
I have seen him again ...

RAOUL
And so our
Phantom's this man ...

GIRY *(starts from her daze and turns to go)*
I have said too much, monsieur.

(She moves off into the surrounding blackness)
And there have been too many accidents ...

RAOUL *(ironical)*
Accidents?!

GIRY
Too many ...

(And before he can question her further, she has disappeared)

RAOUL *(running after her)*
Madame Giry ...!

Scene 3
THE MANAGERS' OFFICE

(The PHANTOM'S score lies open on the desk. ANDRÉ is impatiently flicking through it)

ANDRÉ

**Ludicrous!
Have you seen the score?**

FIRMIN *(entering)*

Simply ludicrous!

ANDRÉ

It's the final straw!

FIRMIN

**This is lunacy!
Well, you know my views ...**

ANDRÉ

Utter lunacy!

FIRMIN

But we daren't refuse ...

ANDRÉ *(groans)*

**Not another
chandelier ...**

FIRMIN

**Look, my friend what
we have here ...**

(He has two notes from the PHANTOM, one of which he hands to ANDRÉ, who opens it and reads):

ANDRÉ

**'Dear André,
Re my orchestrations:
We need another first bassoon.
Get a player with tone –
and that third trombone
has to go!
The man could not be deafer,
so please preferably one
who plays in tune!'**

FIRMIN *(reading his his letter)*

**'Dear Firmin,
vis à vis my opera:
some chorus-members must be sacked.
It you could, find out which
has a sense of pitch –
wisely, though,
I've managed to assign a
rather minor rôle to those
who cannot act!'**

(They are interrupted by the arrival of CARLOTTA and PIANGI, both furiously brandishing similar notes)

CARLOTTA

Outrage!

FIRMIN

What is it now?

CARLOTTA

**This whole affair is
an outrage!**

FIRMIN

Signora, please ...

ANDRÉ

Now what's the matter?

CARLOTTA

**Have you seen
the size of my part?**

ANDRÉ

Signora, listen ...

PIANGI

It's an insult!

FIRMIN

Not you as well!

PIANGI

**Just look at this –
it's an insult!**

FIRMIN

Please, understand ...

ANDRÉ

Signor! Signora!

CARLOTTA
The things I have
to do for my art!

PIANGI *(stabbing a finger at the open score)*
If you can call
this gibberish 'art'!

(RAOUL and CHRISTINE enter. CARLOTTA bristles)

CARLOTTA *(dryly)*
Ah! Here's our little flower!

FIRMIN
Ah, Miss Daaé,
quite the lady
of the hour!

ANDRÉ *(explaining)*
You have
secured the largest rôle
in this 'Don Juan'.

CARLOTTA *(half to herself)*
Christine Daaé?
She doesn't have
the voice!

FIRMIN *(hearing this, to CARLOTTA)*
Signora, please!

RAOUL *(to the MANAGERS)*
Then I take it
you're agreeing.

CARLOTTA *(aside)*
She's behind this . . .

ANDRÉ
It appears we have
no choice.

CARLOTTA *(unable to contain herself any longer, points accusingly)*
She's the one
behind this!
Christine Daaé!

CHRISTINE *(who has been silent till now, incensed at this)*
How dare you!

CARLOTTA
I'm not a fool!

CHRISTINE
You evil woman!
How dare you!

CARLOTTA
You think I'm blind?

CHRISTINE
This isn't *my* fault!
I don't want any
part in this plot!

FIRMIN
Miss Daaé, surely . . .

ANDRÉ
But *why* not?

PIANGI *(baffled, to CARLOTTA)*
What does she say?

FIRMIN *(reasonably)*
It's your decision –

(Suddenly rounding on her)
But *why* not?

CARLOTTA *(to PIANGI)*
She's backing out!

ANDRÉ
You have a duty!

CHRISTINE
I cannot sing it,
duty or not!

RAOUL *(comforting)*
Christine . . .
Christine . . .
You don't have to . . .
they can't make you . . .

(MEG and GIRY arrive, the latter bearing another note from the PHANTOM)

GIRY
Please, monsieur:
another note.

(The MANAGERS gesture: 'read it'. As she reads, ALL react variously, as they are singled out)

GIRY
'Fondest greetings
to you all!
A few instructions,
just before
rehearsal starts:
Carlotta must be
taught to act . . . ,'

(The PHANTOM'S voice gradually takes over from her)

PHANTOM'S VOICE
. . . not her normal trick
of strutting round the stage.
Our Don Juan must
lose some weight –
it's not healthy in
a man of Piangi's age.
And my managers
must learn
that their place is in
an office, not the arts.

As for Miss Christine Daaé . . .
No doubt she'll
do her best – it's
true her voice is
good. She knows, though,
should she wish to excel,
she has much still
to learn, if pride will
let her
return to me, her
teacher,
her teacher . . .

Your obedient friend . . .

(The PHANTOM'S voice fades out and GIRY takes over)

GIRY
'. . . and Angel . . .'

(Attention now focuses on RAOUL, whose eyes are suddenly bright with a new thought)

RAOUL
We have all been
blind – and yet the
answer is staring us
in the face . . .
This could be the
chance to ensnare our
clever friend . . .

ANDRÉ
We're listening . . .

FIRMIN
Go on . . .

RAOUL
We shall play his
game – perform his
work – but remember we
hold the ace . . .
For, if Miss Daaé
sings, he is certain
to attend . . .

ANDRÉ *(carried along by the idea)*
We make certain
the doors are barred . . .

FIRMIN *(likewise)*
We make certain
our men are there . . .

RAOUL
We make certain
they're armed . . .

RAOUL/ANDRÉ/FIRMIN *(savouring their victory)*
The curtain falls –
his reign will end!

(ALL have been listening intently: GIRY is the first to express a reaction. CHRISTINE remains silent and withdrawn)

GIRY
Madness!

ANDRÉ
I'm not so sure . . .

FIRMIN
Not if it works . . .

GIRY
This is madness!

ANDRÉ
The tide will turn!

GIRY
Monsieur, believe me –
there *is* no way of
turning the tide!

FIRMIN *(to GIRY)*
You stick to ballet!

RAOUL *(rounding on GIRY)*
Then help us!

GIRY
Monsieur, I can't...

RAOUL
Instead of warning us...

RAOUL/ANDRÉ/FIRMIN
Help us!

GIRY
I wish I could...

RAOUL/ANDRÉ/FIRMIN
Don't make excuses!

RAOUL
Or could it be that
you're on his side?

GIRY *(to RAOUL)*
Monsieur, believe me,
I intend no ill...

(to ANDRÉ and FIRMIN)

But messieurs, be careful –
we have seen him kill...

ANDRÉ/FIRMIN *(to GIRY)*
We say he'll fall,
and fall he will!

CARLOTTA
She's the one behind this!
Christine!
This is all her doing!

PIANGI
This is the truth!
Christine Daaé!

RAOUL
This is his undoing!

ANDRÉ/FIRMIN *(to RAOUL)*
If you succeed,
you free us all –
this so-called 'angel'
has to fall!

RAOUL
Angel of music,
fear my fury –
Here is where you fall!

GIRY *(to RAOUL)*
Hear my warning!
Fear his fury!

CARLOTTA
What glory can
she hope to gain?
It's clear to all
the girl's insane!

ANDRÉ *(to FIRMIN)*
If Christine sings
we'll get our man...

PIANGI
She is crazy!
She is raving!

FIRMIN *(to ANDRÉ)*
If Christine helps
us in this plan...

RAOUL
Say your prayers,
black angel of death!

CHRISTINE *(vainly pleading amidst the tumult)*
Please don't...

ANDRÉ *(to FIRMIN)*
If Christine won't,
then no one can...

GIRY *(to RAOUL)*
Monsieur, I beg you,
do not do this...

PIANGI/CARLOTTA
Gran Dio!
Che imbroglio!

ANDRÉ/FIRMIN
This will seal his fate!

CHRISTINE *(bursting through the hubbub with a great cry)*
If you don't stop,
I'll go mad!!!

(to RAOUL, pleading)

Raoul, I'm frightened –
don't make me do this...
Raoul, it scares me –
don't put me through this
ordeal by fire...
he'll take me, I know...
we'll be parted for ever...
he won't let me go...

What I once used to dream
I now dread...
if he finds me, it won't
ever end...
and he'll always be there,
singing songs in my head...
he'll always be there,
singing songs in my head...

(ALL stare at her)

CARLOTTA
She's mad...

RAOUL *(to CHRISTINE)*
You said yourself
he was nothing
but a man...

Yet while he lives,
he will haunt us
till we're dead...

(CHRISTINE turns away, unhappily)

CHRISTINE
Twisted every way,
what answer can I give?
Am I to risk my life,
to win the chance to live?
Can I betray the man,
who once inspired my voice?
Do I become his prey?
Do I have any choice?

He kills without a thought,
he murders all that's good...
I know I can't refuse,
and yet, I wish I could...
Oh God – if I agree,
what horrors wait for me
in this, the Phantom's opera...?

RAOUL *(to CHRISTINE, very tenderly)*
Christine, Christine,
don't think that I don't care –
but every hope
and every prayer
rests on you now...

(CHRISTINE, overcome by her conflicting emotions, turns away and hurries out. RAOUL strides forward and addresses an imaginary PHANTOM)

RAOUL
So, it is to be war between us! But this time,
clever friend, the disaster will be yours!

(As lights fade, ATTENDANTS stretch a red, velvet rope across the downstage area. OTHERS bring on gilt chairs. CARLOTTA, PIANGI and GIRY move downstage to take their places for the next scene)

Scene 4
A REHEARSAL FOR 'DON JUAN TRIUMPHANT'
(REYER supervises the learning of the new piece from the piano. Present are PIANGI, CHRISTINE, CARLOTTA, GIRY and CHORUS)

CHORUS
Hide your sword now, wounded knight!
Your vainglorious gasconnade
brought you to your final fight –
for your pride, high price you've paid!
CHRISTINE
Silken couch and hay-filled barn –
both have been his battlefield.
PIAGNI *(wrong)*
Those who tangle with Don Juan...
REYER *(stopping him)*
No, no, no! Chorus – rest, please.

Don Juan, Signor Piangi – here is the phrase.

(He demonstrates it)

'Those who *tangle* with Don Juan...'
If you please?

PIANGI *(still wrong)*
Those who tangle with Don Juan...

REYER
No, no. Nearly – but no.
'Those who *tan, tan, tan*...'

PIANGI *(still wrong)*
Those who tangle with Don Juan...

CARLOTTA *(to the OTHERS)*

His way is better. At least he makes it sound like music!

GIRY *(to CARLOTTA)*

Signora – would you speak that way in the presence of the composer?

CARLOTTA *(deaf to the implications of this remark)*

The composer is not here. And if he *were* here, I would ...

GIRY *(cutting in, ominous)*

Are you certain of that, Signora ... ?

REYER

So, once again – after seven.

(He gives the note and counts in)

Five, six, seven ...

PIANGI *(wrong again)*

Those who tangle with Don Juan ...

(Gradually EVERYONE starts either to talk or to practise the phrase simultaneously)

CARLOTTA

Ah, più non posso! What does it matter what notes we sing?

GIRY

Have patience, Signora.

CARLOTTA

No one will know if it is right, or if it is wrong. No one will *care* if it is right, or if it is wrong.

CARLOTTA *(mocking)*

**Those who tangle
with Don Juan!**

PIANGI *(trying again)*

Those who tan ... tan ...

(to CHRISTINE)

Is right?

CHRISTINE *(to PIANGI)*

Not quite, Signor:
Those who *tan ... tan ...*

REYER *(attempting to restore order)*

Ladies ... Signor Piangi ... if you please ...

*(REYER thumps the piano keys, then leaves the piano, and attempts to attract attention using signals.
At the height of the mayhem, the piano suddenly begins to demonstrate the music unaided. It plays with great force and rhythm. ALL fall silent and freeze, then suddenly start to sing the piece robotically and accurately. As they continue to sing, CHRISTINE moves away from the group)*

ALL EXCEPT CHRISTINE

**Poor young maiden! For the thrill
on your tongue of stolen sweets
you will have to pay the bill –
tangled in the winding sheets!**

(As the ENSEMBLE becomes background, CHRISTINE, transfixed, sings independently):

CHRISTINE

**In sleep
he sang to me,
in dreams
he came ...
that voice
which calls to me
and speaks
my name ...**

(The scene begins to change. Trance-like, CHRISTINE moves slowly upstage. We hear the distant sound of bells)

**Little Lotte
thought of everything and nothing ...
Her father promised her
that he would send her the Angel of
Music ...
Her father promised her ...
Her father promised her ...**

Scene 5
A GRAVEYARD
(A mausoleum with hanging moss. In the centre a pyramid of skulls in front of a cross)

CHRISTINE

**You were once
my one companion ...
you were all
that mattered ...
You were once
a friend and father –
then my world
was shattered ...**

**Wishing you were
somehow here again ...
wishing you were
somehow near ...
Sometimes it seemed,
if I just dreamed,
somehow you would
be here ...**

**Wishing I could
hear your voice again ...
knowing that I
never would ...
Dreaming of you
won't help me to do
all that you dreamed
I could ...**

**Passing bells
and sculpted angels,
cold and monumental,
seem, for you,
the wrong companions –
you were warm and gentle ...**

**Too many years
fighting back tears ...
Why can't the past
just die ... ?**

**Wishing you were
somehow here again ...
knowing we must
say goodbye ...**

**Try to forgive ...
teach me to live ...
give me the strength
to try ...**

**No more memories,
no more silent tears ...
No more gazing across
the wasted years ...
Help me say
goodbye.**

(The PHANTOM emerges from behind the cross)

PHANTOM *(very soft and enticing)*

**Wandering child ...
so lost ...
so helpless ...
yearning for my
guidance ...**

(Bewildered, CHRISTINE looks up, and murmurs breathlessly):

CHRISTINE

**Angel ... or father ...
friend ... or
Phantom ... ?
Who is it there,
staring ... ?**

PHANTOM *(more and more hypnotic)*

**Have you
forgotten your Angel ... ?**

CHRISTINE

**Angel ... oh, speak ...
What endless
longings
echo in this
whisper ... !**

(RAOUL appears in the shadows and watches for a moment, transfixed)

PHANTOM *(now drawing CHRISTINE towards him)*

**Too long you've wandered
in winter ...**

RAOUL *(to himself, a murmur)*

**Once again
she is his ...**

PHANTOM

**Far from my
far-reaching gaze ...**

RAOUL

**Once again
she returns ...**

CHRISTINE *(increasingly mesmerized)*

**Wildly my mind
beats against you ...**

PHANTOM

You resist ...

PHANTOM/CHRISTINE

**Yet your/the soul
obeys ...**

RAOUL
... to the arms
of her angel ...
angel or demon ...
still he calls her ...
luring her back, from the grave ...
angel or dark seducer ...?
Who are you, strange
angel ...?

PHANTOM

Angel of Music!
You denied me,
turning from true beauty ...
Angel of Music!
Do not shun me ...
Come to your strange
Angel ...

CHRISTINE

Angel of Music!
I denied you,
turning from true beauty ...
Angel of Music!
My protector ...
Come to me, strange
Angel ...

(CHRISTINE moves towards the figure of the PHANTOM)

PHANTOM *(beckoning her)*

I am your Angel of Music ...
Come to me: Angel of Music ...

RAOUL *(suddenly calling out)*

Angel of darkness!
Cease this torment!

(Inexorably, the PHANTOM continues to beckon CHRISTINE)

PHANTOM

I am your Angel of Music ...
Come to me: Angel of Music ...

RAOUL *(in desperation)*

Christine! Christine, listen to me!
Whatever you may believe, this man ...
this thing ... is *not* your father!

(to the PHANTOM)

Let her go! For God's sake, *let her go!*
Christine!

(Coming out of her trance, CHRISTINE turns and mouths the word):

CHRISTINE

Raoul, no ...

(She runs to RAOUL, who embraces her protectively. The PHANTOM freezes for a moment and then suddenly seizes a pike, upon which is impaled a skull. At a movement from him, a flash of fire streaks from the gaping mouth of the skull, and lands at RAOUL's feet)

PHANTOM

Bravo, monsieur!
Such spirited words!

(Another fireball)

RAOUL

More tricks, monsieur?

PHANTOM

Let's see, monsieur,
how far you dare go!

(Another fireball)

RAOUL

More deception? More violence?

CHRISTINE *(to RAOUL)*

Raoul, no . . .

(RAOUL has begun to walk, slowly and resolutely, towards the PHANTOM, the fireballs always landing just ahead of him)

PHANTOM

That's right, that's right,
monsieur –
keep walking this way!

(Two more fireballs)

RAOUL

You can't win her love by making her your prisoner.

CHRISTINE

Raoul, don't . . .

RAOUL *(to CHRISTINE)*

Stay back!

PHANTOM

I'm here, I'm here,
monsieur:
the angel of death!
Come on, come on,
monsieur,
Don't stop, don't stop!

*(Three more fireballs.
RAOUL is almost at the PHANTOM's feet. A confrontation is imminent, when CHRISTINE suddenly rushes across to RAOUL)*

CHRISTINE

Raoul! Come back . . .

(She pulls him away)

PHANTOM

Don't go!

(As they are exiting, the PHANTOM declaims in fury):

So be it! Now let it be war upon you *both*!

(At a gesture from the PHANTOM, there is a flash of lighting and the stage erupts into flame)

Scene 6

BEFORE THE PREMIÈRE

THE OPERA HOUSE ON THE NIGHT OF THE PREMIÈRE OF 'DON JUAN TRIUMPHANT'
*(The orchestra is tuning. A whistle sounds – the CHIEF FIRE OFFICER is reviewing two FIRE MARSHALS in tin helmets. A worklight on a stand illuminates them.
Also present are RAOUL, ANDRÉ and FIRMIN, supervising the proceedings, and a MARKSMAN, at present hidden in the pit)*

    CHIEF

    You understand your instructions?

    FIREMEN *(severally)*

    Sir!

CHIEF

When you hear the whistle, take up your positions. I shall then instruct you to secure the doors. It is *essential* that *all* doors are properly secured.

FIRMIN

Are we doing the right thing, André?

ANDRÉ

Have you got a better idea?

CHIEF

Monsieur le Vicomte, am I to give the order?

RAOUL

Give the order.

(The CHIEF blows his whistle. The FIREMEN fan out, leaving RAOUL, the CHIEF and the MANAGERS on stage)

RAOUL *(to the MARKSMAN)*

You in the pit – do you have a clear view of this box?

MARKSMAN *(appearing from the pit)*

Yes, sir.

RAOUL

Remember, when the time comes, shoot. Only if you have to – but shoot. To kill.

MARKSMAN

How will I know, sir?

RAOUL

You'll know.

FIRMIN

Monsieur le Vicomte, are you confident that this will work? Will Miss Daaé sing?

RAOUL

Don't worry, Firmin, André?

ANDRÉ

We're in your hands, sir.

CHIEF

My men are now in position, sir.

RAOUL

Go ahead, then.

(Sounding his whistle again, the CHIEF shouts into the auditorium):

CHIEF

Are the doors secure?

*(Exit doors are slammed all over the building, the FIREMEN answering one by one: 'Secure!'
The orchestra falls silent. Very quietly, from nowhere, we hear the VOICE of the PHANTOM)*

PHANTOM'S VOICE

I'm here: The Phantom of the Opera . . .

(ALL look round apprehensively. FIREMEN start to run in the direction of the VOICE)

PHANTOM'S VOICE *(from somewhere else)*

I'm here: The Phantom of the Opera . . .

*(Again, they follow the VOICE. This happens several times, the PHANTOM'S VOICE darting more and more bewilderingly from place to place. Finally it is heard from Box Five, and in the confusion, the MARKSMAN fires a shot.
RAOUL rounds on the MARKSMAN furiously)*

RAOUL

Idiot! You'll kill someone. I said: only when the time comes!

MARKSMAN

But, Monsieur le Vicomte . . .

(The PHANTOM'S VOICE cuts in, filling the building. All look up)

PHANTOM'S VOICE

No 'buts'! For once, Monsieur Le Vicomte is right . . .
Seal my
fate tonight – I
hate to have to
cut the fun short,
but the joke's
wearing thin . . .
Let the audience in . . .
Let my opera begin!

Scene 7

'DON JUAN TRIUMPHANT'

(The set of the final scene of 'Don Juan Triumphant'. A huge hall with an arch. Behind the arch, which has curtains, is a bed. A fine table, laid for two. PASSARINO, DON JUAN'S servant, is directing the STAFF as they make the room ready. They are a crowd of sixteenth century ruffians and hoydens, proud of their master's reputation as a libertine)

CHORUS

Here the sire may serve the dam,
here the master takes his meat!
Here the sacrificial lamb
utters one despairing bleat!

CARLOTTA AND CHORUS

Poor young maiden! For the thrill
on your tongue of stolen sweets
you will have to pay the bill –
tangled in the winding sheets!

Serve the meal and serve the maid!
Serve the master so that, when
tables, plans and maids are laid,
Don Juan triumphs once again!

(SIGNOR PIANGI, as Don Juan, emerges from behind the arch. MEG, a gypsy dancer pirouettes coquettishly for him. He throws her a purse. She catches it and leaves)

DON JUAN

Passarino, faithful friend,
once again recite the plan.

PASSARINO

Your young guest believes I'm you –
I, the master, you, the man.

DON JUAN

When you met you wore my cloak,
with my scarf you hid your face.
She believes she dines with me,
in her master's borrowed place!
Furtively, we'll scoff and quaff,
stealing what, in truth, is mine.
When it's late and modesty
starts to mellow, with the wine . . .

PASSARINO

You come home! I use your voice –
slam the door like crack of doom!

DON JUAN

I shall say: 'come – hide with me!
Where, oh, where? Of course – my room!'

PASSARINO

Poor thing hasn't got a chance!

DON JUAN

Here's my hat, my cloak and sword.
Conquest is assured,
if I do not forget myself and laugh . . .

*(DON JUAN puts on PASSARINO'S cloak and goes into the curtained alcove where the bed awaits.
Although we do not yet know it, the Punjab Lasso has done its work, and SIGNOR PIANGI is no more. When next we see DON JUAN, it will be the PHANTOM. Meanwhile, we hear AMINTA (CHRISTINE) singing happily in the distance)*

AMINTA (CHRISTINE – *offstage, entering*)

'... no thoughts
within her head.
but thoughts of joy!
No dreams
within her heart,
but dreams of love!'

PASSARINO (*onstage*)

Master?

DON JUAN (*PHANTOM – behind the curtain*)

Passarino – go away!
For the trap is set and waits for its prey ...

*(PASSARINO leaves. CHRISTINE (AMINTA) enters.
She takes off her claok and sits down. Looks about her.
No one. She starts on an apple.
The PHANTOM, disguised as DON JUAN pretending to
be PASSARINO, emerges. He now wears PASSARINO'S
robe, the cowl of which hides his face. His first words
startle her)*

DON JUAN (*PHANTOM*)

You have come here
in pursuit of
your deepest urge,
in pursuit of
that wish,
which till now
has been silent,
silent ...

I have brought you,
that our passions
may fuse and merge –
in your mind
you've already
succumbed to me,
dropped all defences,
completely succumbed to me –
now you are here with me:
no second thoughts,
you've decided,
decided ...

Past the point
of no return –
no backward glances:
the games we've played
till now are at
an end ...
Past all thought
of 'if' or 'when' –
no use resisting:
abandon thought,
and let the dream
descend ...

What raging fire
shall flood the soul?
What rich desire
unlocks its door?
What sweet seduction
lies before
us ...?

Past the point
of no return,
the final threshold –
what warm,
unspoken secrets
will we learn?
beyond the point
of no return ...

AMINTA (*CHRISTINE*)

You have brought me
to that moment
where words run dry,
to that moment
where speech
disappears
into silence,
silence ...

I have come here,
hardly knowing
the reason why ...
In my mind,
I've already
imagined our
bodies entwining,
defenceless and silent –
and now I am
here with you:
no second thoughts,
I've decided,
decided ...

Past the point
of no return –
no going back now:
our passion-play
has now, at last,
begun ...
Past all thought
of right or wrong –
one final question:
how long should we
two wait, before
we're one ...?

When will the blood
begin to race,
the sleeping bud
burst into bloom?
When will the flames,
at last, consume
us ...?

BOTH
Past the point
of no return,
the final threshold –
the bridge
is crossed, so stand
and watch it burn ...
We've passed the point
of no return ...

*(By now the audience and the POLICE have realized that
SIGNOR PIANGI is dead behind the curtain, and it is the
PHANTOM who sings in his place. CHRISTINE knows
it too. As final confirmation, the PHANTOM sings):*

PHANTOM
Say you'll share with
me one
love, one lifetime ...
Lead me, save me
from my solitude ...

*(He takes from his finger a ring and holds it out to her.
Slowly she takes it and puts it on her finger)*

Say you want me
with you,
here beside you ...
Anywhere you go
let me go too –
Christine,
that's all I ask of ...

*(We never reach the word "you", for CHRISTINE quite
calmly reveals the PHANTOM'S face to the audience. As
the FORCES OF LAW close in on the horrifying skull, the
PHANTOM sweeps his cloak around her and vanishes.
MEG pulls the curtain upstage, revealing PIANGI'S body
garrotted, propped against the bed, his head gruesomely
tilted to one side. She screams)*

TRANSFORMATION TO:

*REVERSE VIEW OF THE STAGE (POLICE,
STAGEHANDS, etc. rush onto the stage in confusion.
Also: ANDRÉ, FIRMIN, RAOUL, GIRY, CARLOTTA
and MEG)*

CARLOTTA
What is it? What has happened? Ubaldo!

ANDRÉ
Oh, my God ... my God ...

FIRMIN
We're ruined, André – ruined!

GIRY *(to RAOUL)*
Monsieur le Vicomte! Come with me!

CARLOTTA *(rushing over to PIANGI'S body)*
Oh, my darling, my darling ... who has done
this ...?

(hysterical, attacking ANDRÉ)
You! Why did you let this happen?

*(She breaks down, as PIANGI'S body is carried off on a
stretcher)*

GIRY
Monsieur le Vicomte, I know where they are.

RAOUL
But can I trust you?

GIRY
You must. But remember, your hand at the
level of your eyes!

RAOUL
But why ...?

GIRY
Why? The Punjab lasso, monsieur. First
Buquet. Now Piangi.

MEG *(holding up her hand)*
Like this, monsieur. I'll come with you.

GIRY
No, Meg! No, you stay here!

(to RAOUL)
Come with me, monsieur. Hurry, or we shall
be too late ...

Scene 8
THE LABYRINTH UNDERGROUND

*(Meanwhile, down below, we see the PHANTOM and
CHRISTINE in the boat, crossing the underground
lake)*

PHANTOM *(furiously propelling the boat
onwards)*
Down once more
to the dungeon
of my black despair!
Down we plunge
to the prison
of my mind!
Down that path
into darkness
deep as hell!

(He rounds on her, bitterly)
Why, you ask,
was I bound and chained
in this cold and dismal place?
Not for any
mortal sin, but the
wickedness of
my abhorrent face!

(He hears the offstage voices of the pursuing MOB)

MOB *(offstage)*
Track down this murderer!
He must be found!

PHANTOM *(moving off again)*
Hounded out by
everyone!
Met with hatred
everywhere!
No kind word from
anyone!
No compassion
anywhere!

Christine, Christine ...
Why, why ...?

*(RAOUL and GIRY appear above. They make their way
down, meeting a pack of rats. GIRY screams and lowers
her guard. The rats and the RATCATCHER pass them.
GIRY raises her hand again)*

GIRY
Your hand at the level of your eyes!

RAOUL
... at the level of your eyes ...

MOB *(offstage)*
Your hand at the level of your eyes!

> GIRY
> He lives across the lake, monsieur. This is as far as I dare go.
> RAOUL
> Madame Giry, thank you.

*(She turns to go back up the slope. RAOUL looks at the water. He removes his coat and plunges in.
The MOB appears at the top of the slope. They come down to the lake edge, their torches flickering)*

MOB
Track down this
murderer –
He must be found!
Hunt out this
animal,
who runs to ground!
Too long he's
preyed on us –
but now we know:
the Phantom of the Opera
is there,
deep down below ...

He's here: the Phantom of the Opera ...

(They turn back up the slope. Perhaps there is another way in. The gate to the lair descends, as the rest of the lair appears.)

Scene 9
BEYOND THE LAKE

(The dummy of CHRISTINE sits crumpled on a large throne. The PHANTOM drags CHRISTINE roughly out of the boat. She frees herself and backs away as he stares blackly out front. Braving her terror, she addresses him fiercely).

CHRISTINE
Have you gorged yourself
at last, in your
lust for blood?

(no reply)

Am I now to be
prey to your
lust for flesh?

PHANTOM *(Coldly)*
That fate, which
condemns me
to wallow in blood
has also
denied me
the joys of the flesh ...
this face –
the infection
which poisons our love ...

(He takes the bridal veil from the dummy, and moves slowly towards her)

This face,
which earned
a mother's fear
and loathing ...
A mask,
my first
unfeeling scrap
of clothing ...

(He places the veil on her head)

Pity comes
too late –
turn around
and face your fate:
an eternity of *this*
before your eyes!

(They are almost touching. She looks calmly and coldly into his face)

CHRISTINE
This haunted face
holds no horror
for me now ...
It's in your soul
that the true
distortion lies ...

The PHANTOM suddenly senses RAOUL'S presence. Behind the portcullis, RAOUL climbs out of the water)

PHANTOM
Wait! I think, my dear,
we have a guest!

(to RAOUL)

Sir, this is indeed
an unparalleled delight!
I had rather hoped
that you would come.
And now my wish comes true –
you have truly made my night!

RAOUL *(pleading, grasping the bars of the gate)*
Free her!
Do what you like,
only free her!
Have you no pity?

PHANTOM *(to CHRISTINE, dryly)*
Your lover makes
a passionate plea!

CHRISTINE
Please, Raoul, it's useless ...

RAOUL
I love her!
Does that mean nothing?
I love her?
Show some compassion ...

PHANTOM (snarls furiously at RAOUL)
The world showed no
compassion to me!

RAOUL
Christine ...
Christine ...

(to PHANTOM)

Let me see her ...

PHANTOM (dryly)
Be my guest, sir ...

(He guestured, and the fence rises. RAOUL enters)

Monsieur, I
bid you welcome!
Did you think that
I would harm her?
Why should I make
her pay
for the sins which
are yours?

(So saying, he takes the Punjab lasso and before RAOUL
has a chance to move, catches him by the neck. The end of
the rope, of which the PHANTOM has let go, remains
magically suspended in mid-air)

(taunting)

Order your fine horses now!
Raise up your hand to the level of your
eyes!
Nothing can save you now –
except perhaps Christine ...

(He turns to her)

Start a new life with me –
Buy his freedom with your love!
Refuse me, and you send your lover to his
death!
This is the choice –
This is the point of no return!

CHRISTINE (to the PHANTOM)
The tears I might have shed
for your dark fate
grow cold, and turn to tears
of hate ...

RAOUL (despairing)
Christine, forgive
me, please forgive me ...
I did it all
for you, and all for
nothing ...

CHRISTINE (looking at the PHANTOM, but to
herself)
Farewell,
my fallen idol
and false friend ...
One by one
I've watched
illusions shattered ...

PHANTOM (to CHRISTINE)
To late for
turning back,
too late for
prayers and
useless pity ...

RAOUL (to CHRISTINE)
Say you love him,
and my
life is over!

PHANTOM
Past all hope
of cries for help:
no point in fighting –

RAOUL
Either way
you choose,
he has to win ...

PHANTOM
For either way
you choose,
you cannot win!

So, do you end
your days with me,
or do you send
him to his grave?

RAOUL (to PHANTOM)
Why make her lie
to you, to save
me?

CHRISTINE
Angel of Music ...

PHANTOM
Past the point
of no return –

RAOUL
For pity's sake,
Christine, say no!

CHRISTINE
... why this torment?

PHANTOM
... the final threshold ...

RAOUL
Don't throw your life
away for my sake ...

CHRISTINE
When will you see reason ...?

PHANTOM
His life is now the prize
which you must earn!

RAOUL
I fought so hard
to free you ...

CHRISTINE
Angel of Music ...

PHANTOM
You've passed the point
of no return ...

CHRISTINE
... you deceived me –
I gave my mind
blindly ...

PHANTOM (to CHRISTINE)
You try my patience –
make your choice!

(She reflects for a moment, then with resolution moves
slowly towards the PHANTOM)

CHRISTINE (quietly at first, then with growing
emotion)
Pitiful creature
of darkness ...
What kind of life
have you known ...?

God give me courage
to show you
you are not
alone ...

(Now calmly facing him, she kisses him long and full on
the lips. The embrace lasts a long time. RAOUL watches
in horror and wonder.

The PHANTOM takes a lighted candle and holds it above
RAOUL'S head. A tense moment. But the suspended rope
suddenly falls harmlessly – the PHANTOM has burnt the
thread by which the noose was held. Resigned, he
addresses RAOUL, as we hear the offstage voices of the
approaching MOB)

MOB
Some:
Track down this
murderer –
he must be found!
Hunt out this
animal,
who runs to ground!

Too long he's
preyed on us –
but now we know:
the Phantom of the Opera
is there,
deep down below . . .

Others:
Who is this monster,
this murdering beast?
Revenge for Piangi!
Revenge for Buquet!
This creature
must never go free . . .

PHANTOM
Take her – forget me – forget all of this . . .
Leave me alone – forget all you've seen . . .
Go now – don't let them find you!
Take the boat – leave me here – go now,
don't wait . . .
Just take her and go – before it's too late . . .
Go . . .
Go now – go now and leave me!

*(RAOUL and CHRISTINE move off towards the boat.
The PHANTOM looks mockingly at his mask. The
musical box starts up magically, and he listens to it)*

Masquerade . . .
Paper faces on parade . . .
Masquerade . . .
Hide your face,
so the world will
never find you . . .

*(CHRISTINE re-enters and walks slowly towards him.
She takes off her ring and gives it to the PHANTOM)*

PHANTOM
Christine, I love you . . .

*(She hurries off. The PHANTOM puts the ring on his
finger)*

CHRISTINE *(In the distance, to RAOUL, as the
boat pulls away in the shadow)*
Say you'll share with
me, one
love, one lifetime . . .
say the word
and I will follow you . . .

RAOUL
Share each day with me . . .

CHRISTINE
. . . each night . . .

BOTH
. . . each morning . . .

PHANTOM *(looking after her)*
You alone
can make my song take flight –
it's over now, the music of the night . . .

*(The PHANTOM walks slowly towards the throne. He
takes his place on it, sitting on his cloak.
The MOB including MEG, appears above, climbing
down the portcullis. As the MOB enters the lair, the
PHANTOM wraps his cloak around himself and
disappears.
MEG crosses to the throne and picks up his mask in her
small hand)*

FINIS.

ACKNOWLEDGEMENTS

*M*any people made this book possible, and in spite of the exacting calls of putting on a show, gave their time freely to talk. Gratitude is due to the production team of *The Phantom of the Opera* led by Andrew Lloyd Webber, and including Harold Prince, Cameron Mackintosh, Maria Björnson, Gillian Lynne, David Caddick, Sarah Brightman and of course the Phantom himself, Michael Crawford. Martyn Hayes, Peter Everett, Michael Whiteley, Sue Wilmington, Rose Chandler, Anni Partridge, Peter Shepherd and John Gordon, and especially Bob West and Alan Hatton, all co-operated with backstage interviews. Bridget Hayward and Jane Coleman of the Really Useful Group; Peter Thompson, press representative, Nick Allott and Howard Harrison of Cameron Mackintosh Limited; Anthony Pye-Jeary and Chrissie Hall of DeWynters Limited; Philip Arnott of The Obsession of Dance Company; and the management and staff of Stoll Moss Theatres made the path smooth. Clive Barda exerted his considerable photographic skills with true dedication.

In France, Martine Kahne of the Opéra Library; Jacques Moati, resident photographer of the Opéra House; Lilian Alter of Roger Viollet; Jean Quach, grandson of Gaston Leroux and the Musee D'Orsay press office were especially helpful. In England thanks are due to Peter Haining, Ken Hill, John Earl, John Muir, David Cheshire, the French Institute, the French Cultural Centre, and particularly Celia de Larabbeti who patiently translated much French research.

The staff of Pavilion Books inspired by the unflagging enthusiasm and optimism of their Managing director, Colin Webb performed a miracle, with Helen Sudell calmly handling a schedule many publishers would regard as impossible and Elizabeth Winder working wonders in production. Peter Bridgewater brought skill and polish to the design.

My most personal thanks are due to my agent, Pat White of Deborah Rogers Limited; my wife Frances for patiently easing my insomnia; but most of all to Jane Rice, without whose energy, dedication and professionalism the book could never have happened.

George Perry, Barnes, London July 1987

The paintings on pages 33, 37–42 were reproduced by kind permission of ROBERT HEINDEL.
The Obsession of Dance Company, Stable Gallery, 10 Bellevue Road, Wandsworth Common, London, SW17 7EB Telephone: 01 767 4688 or PO Box 147, Easton, Connecticut 06612, USA Telephone: 203 261 4546

The publishers wish to thank the following copyright holders for their permission to reproduce the illustrations listed below: Bibliotheque Nationale p. 9, 10 (top), 11, 12, 13, 21 (top); Bridgeman Art Library p. 30 (bottom), 31; David Croswaithe p. 81; Noel Gay Artists Limited p. 72 (bottom); Joseph Hope Williams p. 34, 35, 36; The Kobal Collection p. 45, 47, 48, 49, 50, 51, 52 (bottom), 54, 55 (top), 58, 59 (top), 60, 61, 62, 63; Jean Loup Charmet p. 23; Jacques Moati p. 10 (bottom), 17, 18 (right), 19, 20, 21 (bottom); Musee de L'Affiche p. 30 (top); National Film Archive p. 28, 52 (top), 53, 55 (bottom), 57, 59 (bottom); Terry O'Neill p. 88, 89; Morgan and Goodman Ltd p. 70 (bottom); Really Useful Company P.L.C. p. 68; Reunion des Musees Nationaux p. 25, 27; TyneWear Theatre Company p. 69; Roger Viollet p. 7, 14, 15, 16, 18 (left), 24. All production photography was by Clive Barda.

Original *Phantom of the Opera* graphics which appear on the jacket were designed by DeWynters Limited, and the illustrations by Marcus Bradbury and Dean Hood which appear in the Libretto section were reproduced by kind permission of DeWynters Limited, London. Copyright © The Really Useful Group P.L.C.

CREATIVE TEAM

MUSIC BY ANDREW LLOYD WEBBER
LYRICS BY CHARLES HART

ADDITIONAL LYRICS BY RICHARD STILGOE, BOOK BY RICHARD STILGOE AND ANDREW LLOYD WEBBER
PRODUCTION DESIGN BY MARIA BJÖRNSON, LIGHTING BY ANDREW BRIDGE
SOUND BY MARTIN LEVAN, PRODUCTION MUSICAL SUPERVISION DAVID CADDICK
MUSICAL DIRECTION MICHAEL REED, ORCHESTRATIONS BY DAVID CULLEN AND ANDREW LLOYD WEBBER
MUSICAL STAGING AND CHOREOGRAPHY BY GILLIAN LYNNE
DIRECTED BY HAROLD PRINCE

THE ORIGINAL CAST, ORCHESTRA AND PRODUCTION CREDITS

The Phantom of the Opera	MICHAEL CRAWFORD	PERRY MONTAGUE-MASON	*Leader*
*Christine Daaé**	SARAH BRIGHTMAN	GEOFFREY GREY	*Violin 1*
Raoul, Vicompte De Chagny	STEVE BARTON	ALISON KELLY	*Violin 2*
Monsieur Firmin	JOHN SAVIDENT	MARK BERROW	*Violin 3*
Monsieur Andre	DAVID FIRTH	MARK THOMAS	*Violin 4*
Carlotta Guidicelli	ROSEMARY ASHE	GORDON BUCHAN	*Violin 5*
Madame Giry	MARY MILLAR	FRANCES WALKER	*Violin 6*
Ubaldo Piangi	JOHN ARON	BRIAN MACK	*Viola*
Monsieur Reyer	PAUL ARDEN-GRIFFITH	LINDA COURT	*Viola*
Auctioneer	BARRY CLARK	JUSTIN PEARSON	*Cello*
Porter	DAVID DE VAN	ROBERT NORRIS	*Cello*
Meg Giry	JANET DEVENISH	DAVID ROSE	*Bass Guitar*
Monsieur LeFèvre	DAVID JACKSON	SHEILA BROMBERG	*Harp*
Joseph Buquet	JANOS KURUCZ	ALEXA TURPIN	*Flute/Piccolo*
Don Attilio/Passarino	JAMES PATERSON	CHRIS GRADWELL	*Flute/Clarinet/Saxophone*
Slave Master (in 'Hannibal')	PETER BISHOP	KEITH MARSHALL	*Oboe/Cor Anglais*
Flunky/Stagehand	JUSTIN CHURCH	STEVE PIERCE	*Clarinet/Bass Clarinet/Eb Clarinet*
Policeman	MOSTYN EVANS	PETER WHITTAKER	*Bassoon*
Page (in 'Don Juan Triumphant')	SUE FLANNERY	NORMAN ARCHIBALD	*Trumpet*
Porter/Fireman	ANDREW GOLDER	HOWARD EVANS	*Trumpet*
Page (in 'Don Juan Triumphant')	JANET HOWD	RICHARD WALL	*Trombone*
Wardrobe Mistress	PEGGY ANN JONES	MICHAEL DERE	*Horn*
Princess (in 'Hannibal')	MARIA KESSELMAN	DANIEL EMOND	*Horn*
Madam Firmin	PATRICIA RICHARDS	KEITH RIBY	*Horn*
Innkeeper's Wife		DAVID LOCKE	*Percussion*
(in 'Don Juan Triumphant')	JILL WASHINGTON	PAUL MAGUIRE	*Keyboards*
The Ballet Chorus of the Opera Populaire	SALLY ASHFIELD	MIKE STANLEY	*Keyboards*
	LYNN JEZZARD		
	NICOLA KEEN		
	PATRICIA MERRIN		
	NAOMI TATE		
	ALISON TOWNSEND		
Ballet Swing	DINAH JONES		
**Christine Alternate*	CLAIRE MOORE		

		Company Manager	ROBERT M. WEST
Assistant to Mr Prince	RUTH MITCHELL	*Stage Manager*	ALAN HATTON
Assistant to Miss Lynne	ANN ALLAN	*Deputy Stage Manager*	ANNI PARTRIDGE
Assistant to Designer	JONATHAN ALLEN	*Assistant Stage Managers*	LYNDA WINTON, PHILIP DEVERILL
Costume Co-ordinator	SUE WILMINGTON	*Wardrobe Mistress*	ROSE CHANDLER
Resident Director	GEOFFREY FERRIS	*Wig Supervisor*	PETER KING
Production Manager	MARTYN HAYES	*Sound Operator*	RICHARD SHARRATT
	OF THE PRODUCTION OFFICE	*Console Operator*	ALAN MATIESON